*To Sandra*

# Let us sing to the Lord!

*with all good wishes*

## Hymns for use during the Christian Year

*with love "in Christ"*

### By

### John L. Forster

*John*

British Library Cataloguing in Publication Data.
A catalogue record for this book is available
from the British Library.

ISBN 978 0 86071 832 1

MOORLEYS
Print, Design & Publishing
info@moorleys.co.uk · www.moorleys.co.uk

*Thank you to the team at Moorleys for enabling this publication to happen.*

The hymn-texts in this book are part of my collection of 'Hymns for the Christian Year' written over the last forty-five years of Circuit ministry in the Methodist Church and now numbering upwards of 600 texts. The majority have been used in Sunday worship in Methodist Churches in the Bilston, Milton Keynes, Manchester (North) & Middleton and the Manchester Circuits. Some have been written for special occasions, such as the Marriage Ceremonies of our two daughters in 2003, a 25th Wedding Anniversary, the Baptism of two granddaughters and a grandson and several Church Centenaries and longer 150th and 450th anniversaries in local Anglican Churches. 20 were included by the editor of the excellent *Worship Live,* printed by Stainer and Bell, and feature now on the *HymnQuest* database. The worship sheets I produce Sunday by Sunday obviously find their way into many places and I have received requests to use my material from as far away as the North East and New Zealand. It is good to know that they have crossed the denominational boundaries too – for the hymn is a most ecumenical of instruments in the great panoply of Christian worship materials and resources.

But first, I have to make a confession. I am not a musician, so there are no original musical accompaniments to the texts. I am totally dependent on the tunes included in the past and current hymnbooks in use by churches in this country. It will be a disappointment and seen as a weakness by musicians but I would hope that anyone who feels the urge to rush into composition will go ahead and do so. I wish I had kept both the texts and the music for some of the hymns composed during my ministry in Milton Keynes. Two of our young organists [would that we were able to say that in 2020] produced several original tunes to accompany my words and the choir leader was always really helpful with her comments. With the advent of the personal computer age, storage of worship materials is now much easier and bits of paper do not get lost or mislaid. In more recent times, several church organists have composed tunes for hymns or advised me on a more suitable tune to fit a particular text and two Manchester Circuit Methodist Local Preachers, Ken Whittaker and Clyde Parkin, have been very supportive in this whole endeavour.

I am making this selection of texts available in response to the many people who have enquired after copies following worship occasions. I do so reluctantly because I do not see myself as a poet in the great succession of hymn-writers. The great put-down was when a member of one of my more recent congregations, who thought anything written after 1900 was not worthy of use, said: 'Who do you think you are, Charles Wesley?' He didn't mean it as a complement. I have no pretensions in that direction at all. John Bell, a modern 'great' among hymn-writers, in his book' *The Singing Thing'* gives some clear advice to budding hymn-writers: 'Don't!' Since I started writing hymns long before he published any of the Iona texts, and certainly before I read his book, I have the temerity to press on as a humble 'word smith' who just likes singing.

Hymn-writing is not just a poetic exercise but it is more of a devotional experience for me; a way of expressing the theology that underpins my calling as a presbyter in the Church of Christ and a way of expressing the worship we offer to God – the 'high-calling of the Church of Christ'. I am after all a Methodist, taken to church at three-weeks old to meet my mother's Sunday School class during the latter part of the World War II. So, I have been hearing and singing hymns for a very long time and John Wesley did say "Methodism was born in song".

So, enjoy the singing. I hope that these words will bring a sense of the presence of God in worship if you choose to use them, and that they will enrich such occasions. If they achieve that then their work is done and God is praised and his Name is glorified.

I must express my sincere thanks to all those in Methodism and the wider Church who have been so supportive and encouraging over the years, particularly church organists and choir leaders. Your musical knowledge has been invaluable to me. My wife, Jennifer, partners together in love, life and faith for over fifty years, has shared this exercise from my very first attempts and she has put up my disappearing into the study to jot the latest thoughts down on paper. She has been my greatest encourager and has my special thanks and love.

**John Forster**
**Higher Blackley,**
**Manchester**
**February 2020**

# Contents

# The Church at Worship
## We Gather in God's Presence

1    Lord, we are gathered in this place

2    God, whose glory fills the skies

3    Light and life and joy are found

4    Sunday is the first day

5    O Living God we come to you

6    Ground of being, source of light

7    Come together all God's people

8    Come raise your voices, sing your song

9    Come let us all sing praise to God

10   Sing a song of joy and gladness

11   Lift up your voices

12   Hear the sound of people singing

13   We praise you, O God

14   O Living God, we gather here to worship

15   O Holy God, you spoke at the beginning

16   How shall we worship you, O Lord

# 1. Lord, we are gathered in this place

1. Lord, we are gathered in this place,
   your Name to praise and glorify;
   We come, the people born of grace,
   your gifts receive, your love apply;
   Lord, see the joy upon each face,
   your Name we raise and magnify.

2. Incarnate Lord, in life and love
   you made a covenant anew;
   We come in faith and hope and love,
   our covenant with God renew;
   Meet with us here, Word from above,
   and once again make all things new.

3. We gather round your table, Lord:
   to celebrate your sacred meal;
   Invited through your living Word,
   in bread and wine your life reveal;
   You put yourself into each hand,
   as here our love and life we seal.

4. So, gracious Lord, we sing your praise
   as round your table here we meet;
   We gather here, Lord of all days,
   our faith renew, your food to eat;
   Lord, bless this time of joyful praise,
   as we the songs of heav'n repeat.

5. Then send us out into your world,
   and help us witness to your fame;
   See how love's banner flies unfurled,
   a cross of death, love's sign became;
   Lord, we'll go out into your world,
   we'll show your love and speak your Name.

TUNE: 88.88.88.                    Mozart
Wolfgang Amadeus Mozart (1756-1791)
[Hymns & Psalms 788(i)]
[Singing the Faith 546]

# 2 God, whose glory fills the heavens

1. God, whose glory fills the heavens,
   reigns supreme in time and space;
   Human life and nature sharing,
   God now has a human face.
   Raise your voices!
   Sing God's praises!
   Celebrate his saving grace,
   sing for joy, of love unending,
   given to the human race.

2. Jesus Christ, our friend and brother,
   born among us on the earth;
   Sharing earthly joys and sorrows,
   from the moment of your birth.
   Raise your voices!
   Sing God's praises!
   Celebrate his life on earth,
   through his cross and resurrection
   brought about mankind's rebirth.

3. Holy Spirit, life and power,
   mind and matter permeate;
   Source of all God's gifts and graces,
   love in action radiate.
   Raise your voices!
   Sing God's praises!
   Celebrate a love so great!
   Poured upon Christ's faithful people –
   Christ-likeness in each create.

4.   God creates a faithful people;
     those who follow Christ his Son;
     Through the Holy Spirit working
     in the lives by sin undone.
     Raise your voices!
     Sing God's praises!
     Celebrate what God has done.
     Draw your family together -
     boys and girls and ev'ryone.

5.   As your family in Jesus,
     Lord, we join to speak your praise;
     Words and music flow together
     in this seamless hymn we raise.
     Raise your voices!
     Sing God's praises!
     Celebrate his endless days!
     Come together, sing his glory
     in this hymn of love and praise.

**TUNE: 87.87.D**                    **Ode to Joy**
**Ludwig van Beethoven (1770-1837)**
**[Hymns Old & New revised130]**
**[Singing the Faith 8]**

# 3  Light and life and joy are found

1.  Light and life and joy are found
    In your presence all abound:
    Light forever on us shine;
    Fill each one with life divine;
    Joy unspeakable!

2.  Praise we offer, and love too,
    In your service clear and true:
    Now as one our voices raise
    In our offering of praise;
    Love unspeakable!

3.  Faith and hope and love we bring
    In your fellowship to sing:
    Faith in Christ the living way;
    Love to live each blessed day;
    Hope unspeakable!

4.  Light and praise and faith all shine
    In your love they all combine:
    Light to follow where Christ leads;
    Praise him now in words and deeds;
    Faith unspeakable!

5.  Glory to you, Lord, we bring,
    Praise to Jesus, Christ and King,
    Blessed Holy Spirit true,
    Human voices worship you:
    God unspeakable!

**TUNE: ORIENTIS PARTIBUS 77.77.4.**
**Medieval French Melody arr. Ralph Vaughan Williams (1872-1958)**
**[Hymns & Psalms 168]**
**[Singing the Faith 326]**

# 4   Sunday is the first day

1.   Sunday is the first day
Of the Christian week;
Day of resurrection
Day of Easter joy.
Sunday is the first day
Hearts and tongues employ –
In Christ's name we worship
Share the Easter joy.

2.   Sunday is the first day
Of the Christian week;
Gather at Christ's table,
Feed on bread and wine.
Sunday is the first day
With the Lord we dine –
Join the first disciples,
Sharing Christ's new wine.

3.   Sunday is the first day
Of the Christian week;
Love and worship offer
As God's Name we praise.
Sunday is the first day
Hearts and voices raise;
Join together singing
Offer God our praise.

4.     Sunday is the first day
Of the Christian week;
Time to speak and listen,
Offer and receive.
Sunday is the first day –
Worship and believe,
Gathered here together
God's good gifts receive.

5.     Sunday is the first day
Of the Christian week;
Day of praise and worship
Gathered in Christ's Name.
Sunday is the first day –
Celebrate God's fame
As we join together,
Praise his holy Name.

**TUNE: 6.5.6.5. D**        **Evelyns**
**William Monk (1823-89)**
**[Hymns & Psalms 74(i)]**
**[Singing the Faith 317(ii)]**
**[Mission Praise Combined 600]**

**When the Eucharist is not being celebrated, verse 2 can be omitted.**

# 5    O Living God we come to you

1.    O living God we come to you
      our hearts and voices raise:
      With mind and heart and spirit true
      we join to sing your praise.
      In Jesu's Name we gather here –
      the Spirit's power to know –
      in words and songs his name revere –
      to you our praises flow.

2.    Lord Jesus, take the things we say –
      in songs and readings too;
      Take all the words we speak and pray
      that they may honour you.
      The praise we offer, Lord, receive,
      we of your glory sing;
      We celebrate what we believe
      our praise and worship bring.

3.    Lord, see your table is prepared –
      your own invited guests.
      We will receive the broken bread
      your presence manifests.
      The cup of wine for all to share,
      your cup of blessing know.
      As we all share this holy food –
      let love within us grow.

4.    O may we walk with you each day –
      your presence know and feel?
      Lead us, O Lord, along life's way
      your pilgrim path reveal.
      So, Lord, we give ourselves to you
      in worship and in praise;
      all that we are we offer you –
      your name on high we raise!

**TUNE: DCM.**                    **Soll 'S Sein**
**Melody from D. G. Corner [1649]**
**Arranged by John Wilson [1905 – 1922]**
**[Hymns & Psalms 8]**
**[Singing the Faith 53]**
**When Holy Communion is not included in the Service, verse 3 can be omitted.**

# 6   Ground of being, source of light

1.  Ground of being, source of light,
    energy so infinite;
    through all things you permeate
    shape and order and create.

2.  Out of nothing, let things be,
    processes so full and free;
    Energy in boundless forms,
    creating its own new norms.

3.  Life bursts forth, organic style,
    time's long aeons, takes a while,
    through a diverse, complex mix,
    patterned the double helix.

4.  Human beings take the stage,
    life has reached an advanced age;
    consciousness, awareness too,
    reaching out, good Lord, to you.

5.  Christ, in whom all things cohere,
    hidden God who draws so near;
    working thorough the pow'r of love,
    meaning, purpose here you prove.

6.  So, we share your purpose, Lord,
    great Creator, pow'rful Word;
    here in love we worship you,
    work with Christ in all we do.

**TUNE: 77.77.**                    **Vienna**
**J. H. Knecht (1752-1817)**
**[Hymns & Psalms 764]**
**[Singing the Faith 676]**

# 7   Come together all God's people

1. Come together all God's people,
   bring your worship and your praise;
   in his fellowship to gather,
   hearts on fire and souls ablaze.
   *With full voice his love proclaim.*
   *Lift on high the blessed Name.*

2. Come together all God's people,
   gather here to hear his Word;
   hear the words and acts of Jesus,
   pow'rful teacher, gracious Lord.
   *With full voice his love proclaim.*
   *Lift on high the blessed Name.*

3. Come together all God's people,
   gather round his table spread;
   here he meets you, here he feeds you,
   with love risen from the dead.
   *With full voice his love proclaim.*
   *Lift on high the blessed Name.*

4. Come together all God's people,
   wear your new clothes of his love;
   let his Spirit clothe your praises,
   all his love and goodness prove.
   *With full voice his love proclaim*
   *Lift on high the blessed Name.*

5. Come together all God's people,
   he will send you out to serve,
   in the world through costly service,
   share his love without reserve.
   *With full voice his love proclaim*
   *Lift on high the blessed Name.*

TUNE: 8.7.8.7.77.                    Irby
Henry J. Gauntlett (1805-76)
[Hymns & Psalms 114]
[Singing the Faith 214 & 220]

# 8   Come raise your voices, sing your song

1. Come raise your voices, sing your song,
   to celebrate what God has done;
   the One who brought all things to be,
   a universe of life set free.

2. Tell all who hear, sing out your praise,
   that God is good in all his ways;
   who as a human child was born
   upon the holy Christmas morn.

3. Tell of the child and of the man,
   carpenter, teacher, who began
   to speak of God who could be known
   by all his people, ev'ryone

4. Sing out your song of love proclaimed.
   a Gospel for the unredeemed;
   tell of the way in which he died,
   a cruel death, for all love tried.

5. Then raise your voices loud and clear,
   to sing of Easter, let all hear
   about the one who died, who lives
   and to his people new life gives.

6. Come raise your voices, sing your song,
   of praise and glory to God's Son;
   to God the Father sing your praise,
   sing in the Spirit all your days.

TUNE: 88.88. L.M.   Gonfalon Royal
P. C. Buck (1871-1947)
[Hymns & Psalms 179 / 211]
[Singing the Faith 669]

# 9 Come let us all sing praise to God

1. Come let us all sing praise to God,
   for he is life's Creator;
   the twinkling stars and planets too,
   sky, land and sea and weather;
   each plant and creature, me and you –
   of all he is the maker too:
   to God be praise and glory.

2. Come join the song, sing praise to God,
   for he is life's Sustainer;
   the air we breathe and water too,
   all that we know and measure;
   the things that grow, providing food –
   he creates all and it is good:
   to God be praise and glory.

3. Come gather round, sing praise to God,
   for he is life's Redeemer;
   a baby cries, the Christ is born,
   and God becomes our neighbour;
   to share in all that life can be,
   to show the way and set things free:
   to God be praise and glory.

4.    Come raise your voice, sing praise to God,
    he sends the Holy Spirit;
    the power of God at Pentecost,
    of love beyond all limit;
    so all who speak in the Lord's Name
    his word of love they will proclaim:
    to God be praise and glory.

5.    Come gather all, sing praise to God,
    for he is life's Creator;
    he came to stay in Jesus Christ
    of all he is the Saviour;
    he lives in all through Pentecost,
    to love and serve at countless cost:
    to God be praise and glory.

**TUNE: 8.7.8.7.88.7   Mit Freuden Zart**
**Later form of melody in Bohemian Brethren *Kirchengesang* 1566**
**[Hymns & Psalms 511]**
**[Singing the Faith 117]**

# 10 Sing a song of joy and gladness

1. Sing a song of joy and gladness,
   to the One who lets things be;
   Mother, Father of creation,
   all that we can know and see.
   ***Sing your praises, sing with gladness,***
   ***to the Holy One, the Lord;***
   ***raise your voices, sing with boldness,***
   ***to the first and final Word.***

2. Sing to God who came in Jesus,
   here among us on the earth;
   love alive in words and actions,
   from the cross raised to new birth.
   ***Sing your praises, sing with gladness,***
   ***to the Holy One, the Lord;***
   ***raise your voices, sing with boldness,***
   ***to the first and final Word.***

3. Sing to God the Holy Spirit,
   love at work in you and me;
   life and power, joy and freedom,
   setting captive sinners free.
   ***Sing your praises, sing with gladness,***
   ***to the Holy One, the Lord;***
   ***raise your voices, sing with boldness,***
   ***to the first and final Word.***

4. Sing a song of joy and gladness,
   to the One in Trinity;
   God the Parent, Son and Spirit,
   three in one, in unity.
   ***Sing your praises, sing with gladness,***
   ***to the Holy One, the Lord;***
   ***raise your voices, sing with boldness,***
   ***to the first and final Word.***

TUNE: 87.87.D                    Ode to Joy
Ludwig van Beethoven (1770-1837)
[Hymns Old & New Revised 183]
[Singing the Faith 8]
[Mission Praise Combined 600]

# 11 Lift up your voices

1.    Lift up your voices, let them swell in praise,
the Name above all other names to raise.
***Sing out with joy, for Jesus is the Lord,***
***tell all the world of Christ the living Word.***

2.    Lift up your voices, let them sing a song,
of him to whom all that we know belongs.
***Sing out with joy, for Jesus is the Lord,***
***tell all the world of Christ the living Word.***

3.    Lift up your voices, let them dance for joy,
in songs of praise all music to employ.
***Sing out with joy, for Jesus is the Lord,***
***tell all the world of Christ the living Word.***

4.    Lift up your voices, let them all display
the unity of people of the Way.
***Sing out with joy, for Jesus is the Lord,***
***tell all the world of Christ the living Word.***

TUNE: 10.10.10.10.     Woodlands
Walter Greatorex (1877-1949
[Hymns & Psalms 86]
[Singing the Faith 186]
[Mission Praise Combined 631(ii)]

# 12  Hear the sound of people singing

1.  Hear the sound of people singing,
    praise rings out across the earth,
    it's the Jesus people bringing
    praise to God, they hail his worth.

2.  Join the Jesus people singing,
    let your voice sing out with joy,
    all your gifts and graces bringing,
    to God's praise your gifts employ.

3.  So the many voices singing
    echo praise around the earth,
    day and night the sound is ringing,
    God be praised by all on earth.

4.  Now we join the people singing
    as we praise God's holy Name,
    in our worship praises bringing,
    all our love for God proclaim.

**TUNE: 8.7.8.7.**                    **Adoration**
**J. Eric Hunt (1903-58)**
**[Hymns & Psalms 167]**

**TUNE: 8.7.8.7.**                    **All For Jesus**
**J. Stainer (1840-1901)**
**[Hymns & Psalms 251]**
**[Singing the Faith 341 / 382]**

## 13 We praise you, O God

1.  We praise you, O God, for all you have made,
    all that we can see in grandeur displayed;
    the stars and the planets, the music of spheres,
    a source of great wonder in which all coheres.

2.  We praise you, O God, for coming in Christ,
    a life that you shared, your gift of great price;
    for thought and for action, for love, trust and care,
    for worship and service in which we can share.

3.  We praise you, O God, you show forth your love,
    the Spirit is come through wind, fire and dove;
    to bless Christ's disciples, his cross gladly bear,
    through life and through living your love we declare.

4.  We praise you, O God, for your gifts of grace,
    each given to all, the whole human race;
    you call us to service, all love's fruits to bear,
    to mirror in our lives, your love and your care.

5.  We praise you, O God, the one we adore;
    our Lord and true friend, with whom we explore
    the human condition, life's meaning and ways,
    the way of Christ-likeness through all of our days.

**TUNE: 10.10.11.11.**           **Houghton**
**Henry J. Gauntlett (1805-76)**
**[Hymns & Psalms 504]**

## 14 O Living God, we gather here to worship

1.    O Living God, we gather here to worship
the One who called a universe to be;
meet with us now as we draw near to praise you,
you are the One to set the whole world free.

2.    We recognize your majesty around us,
the splendour of the rising sun at dawn;
the birdsong welcoming the coming daylight,
your life and love proclaimed anew each morn.

3.    Yet in a baby's cry we hear you speaking,
the Word of God, come here to dwell on earth;
you came in Jesus to be one among us,
the One who brought the universe to birth.

4.    Yours, Lord, is the true breath of life within us,
the living Spirit, tongue and dove and flame;
come to inspire us, comfort us and guide us,
that people may your love and life proclaim.

5.    O Living God, we gather here to praise you,
for you have called in Jesus Christ our Lord;
we offer all we are and all we do here,
the servants of your Son, the living Word.

TUNE: 11.10.11.10.  Lord of the Years
Michael Baughen (b. 1930)
Arranged by David Iliff (b. 1939)
[Singing the Faith 470]
[Hymns Old & New Revised 454]
[Mission Praise Combined 428]

# 15 O Holy God, you spoke at the beginning

1. O Holy God, you spoke at the beginning,
   when out of nothing you brought all to be;
   the wonders of the universe around us,
   a touch of glory in all that we see.

2. O Holy Spirit, moving on the waters,
   establishing Creation's rules and norms;
   you dance to the music of God's love and light,
   sustaining life in all its myriad forms.

3. O Word made flesh, in Jesus, dwelling with us,
   the One at whose name every knee will bow;
   the One who calls us to your kingdom journey,
   and bids us join him on that journey now.

4. O Jesus Christ, our Lord, our friend, our brother,
   you journeyed to the Cross, through death to life;
   we hear your call and take our cross up with you,
   so may be join you in your Easter life?

5. O Holy God, we gather in the Spirit,
   the friends of Jesus, met to worship you;
   may we know here the blessing of your presence,
   now as we worship and in all we do?

6. Praise be to God, the life-creating Father,
   and praise to Jesus, the life-giving Son;
   let praise be given to the Holy Spirit,
   O Holy God, eternal, Three in One.

TUNE: 11.10.11.10.          Highwood
Richard Runciman Terry [1865-1838]
[Hymns & Psalms 236]
[Singing the Faith 3]
[Hymns Old & New Revised 227]

# 16   How shall we worship you, O Lord

1.   How shall we worship you, O Lord,
     the maker of the universe;
     How can we reach out with our praise,
     the vastness of space-time traverse?

2.   We'll gather here in Jesu's Name,
     disciples still, his love proclaim;
     We'll do the things he asked us to
     around his table, still the same.

3.   In songs of love, of faith we'll sing,
     the story of his life we'll tell;
     In words and actions follow him,
     Lord, may your Spirit with us dwell.

4.   We'll break the bread and share the cup,
     the symbols of his life receive;
     We'll recognise him as we eat,
     the Easter story we believe.

5.   In Jesu's Name we'll live and serve,
     in our world Jesus calls us still;
     In acts of love and sacrifice
     we'll live our worship, do his will.

6.   Receive our worship, holy God,
     the source of all we see and know;
     Receive our praise, through Jesus Christ,
     the Spirit's gifts of love bestow.

TUNE: 88.88. L.M.                    Old 100th
Melody from Genevan Psalter 1551
[Hymns & Psalms 1] [Singing the Faith 1]

TUNE: 88.88. L.M.                    Martham
J. H. Maunder (1858-1920)
[Hymns & Psalms 42]
[Mission Praise Combined 514]
There are many suitable tunes in this metre.

# The Ministry of Jesus and Our Response

## 17  Can you hear his voice still calling

1.  Can you hear his voice still calling,
    "Will you come and follow me;
    will you share what I am doing,
    ears to hear and eyes to see?"
    *Lord, I hear you calling to me*
    *and I want to follow you;*
    *may your Spirit lead and guide me,*
    *help me share the things you do.*

2.  Jesus, servant of the servants,
    he invites you, 'Join my band';
    come and join, sisters and brothers
    come with me, come take my hand.

3.  Jesus holds his hand out to you,
    take it as he welcomes you;
    offer him the things you can do,
    he will make them all anew.

4.  He invites you to his table,
    come and share his bread and wine;
    he will show you, you are able
    to fish too so all can dine.

5.  He sends you to friends and strangers
    as disciples here on earth;
    gather all as brothers, sisters,
    to his kingdom of new birth.

6.  Can you hear him calling to you?
    His is a persistent call.
    Take the love he offers to you,
    share it now with one and all.
    *Lord, I hear you calling to me*
    *and I want to follow you;*
    *may your Spirit lead and guide me,*
    *as I walk this way with you.*

**TUNE: 87.87.87.87**         Ode to Joy
Ludwig van Beethoven (1770-1827)
[Singing the Faith 81]
[Mission Praise Combined 600]

**TUNE: 87.87.87.87**         Scarlet Ribbons
Evelyn Danzig (1906-1996)
Arranged by John L. Bell (b. 1949)
[Singing the Faith 131]

**TUNE: 87.87.87.87**         Hyfrydol
Rowland Huw Prichard (1811-1887)
Harmonised by Compilers of *English Hymnal*, 1906 [Singing the Faith 103]
[Mission Praise Combined 226, 315]

## 18  Walking in the Christian way
**The Christian life and Christ's presence**

1.   Walking in the Christian way
     is a challenge day by day;
     knowing what to do or say
     at each turn along the way.

     *Where you walk I'll walk with you,*
     *where you are I'll be there too;*
     *when you face things, old or new,*
     *I'll be there to see you through.*

2.   As we worship God above,
     as we reach out here in love,
     in the Spirit, fire and dove,
     one the praise, below, above.

3.   We can hear your call today,
     calling us to take the way,
     live and love, trust and obey,
     and serve Christ the Lord today.

     *Where you walk I'll walk with you,*
     *where you are I'll be there too;*
     *when you face things, old or new,*
     *I'll be there to see you through.*

4. When the times are hard and dry,
   when we fail or aim too high,
   we know that you hear our cry,
   wounds are healed and tears are dry.

5. So we'll travel on good Lord,
   as we serve the living Word;
   may the still small voice be heard,
   as we follow Christ the Lord.

   *Where you walk I'll walk with you,*
   *where you are I'll be there too;*
   *when you face things, old or new,*
   *I'll be there to see you through.*

**TUNE: 77.77**          Lauds [HP326]
**John Whitridge Wilson (1905-92)**
**[Hymns & Psalms 326]**
**[Singing the Faith 398]**

The chorus used after verses 1, 3 & 5 could be sung by a cantor or soloist
standing in another part of the Church, echoing the promise of Christ.

# 19 Touch us with your blessing, Lord

1. Touch us with your blessing, Lord,
   fill us with your love each day;
   through the Spirit be our guide,
   as we travel on life's way.

2. And when things are hard to take,
   life's a mess, darkness abounds;
   may we know your blessing then,
   when love's barque has run aground.

3. In darkness of the night,
   all our hopes seem at an end;
   even when you don't feel near,
   you are there, our constant friend.

4. Touch us with your blessing, Lord,
   alongside us hour by hour;
   you will see us through we know,
   we will trust your love and power.

**TUNE: 77.77.**                    **Vienna**
**J. H. Knecht (1752-1817)**
**[Hymns & Psalms 764]**
**[Singing the Faith 676]**

## 20  Jesus is on a journey

1.  Jesus is on a journey,
    his mission to fulfil;
    as teacher, preacher, healer,
    submitting to God's will.
    A manger to the desert,
    the desert to a cross,
    the cross into a garden,
    love's nature comes across.

2.  To those who feared God's anger,
    another side he showed;
    he brought them loving-kindness,
    God's love just overflowed.
    The crippled, lame and helpless,
    their life and hopes restored;
    he showed them each God's blessing,
    all loved and not ignored.

3.  To all the poor and hopeless,
    good news, the Lord proclaimed;
    be brought them hope and value,
    God knew them all by name.
    The people gathered round him,
    his words were life to them,
    his parables and stories
    each one a unique gem.

4. So, living Lord, we gather,
   your people still today;
   you bring us life and healing
   as we serve you each day.
   A manger to the desert,
   the desert to a cross,
   the cross into a garden,
   love's nature comes across.

5. We journey on with you, Lord,
   we follow where you lead;
   in all things, we will serve you
   and meet you in each need.
   For you are all around us,
   incarnate still today;
   you lead your people onward,
   their life and truth and Way.

**TUNE: 7.6.7.6.D.**                    **Aurelia**
**Samuel Sebastian Wesley (1810-1876)**
**[Hymns & Psalms 515]**
**[Singing the Faith 690]**
**[Mission Praise Combined 126, 640]**

# 21 Hands reach to the stranger

1. Hands reach to the stranger,
   a welcome to extend;
   a handshake crosses many miles
   to greet a new found friend.

2. Hands held up in warning
   of danger, threat or strife,
   can help to save man, woman, child
   from things that could claim life.

3. Hands bunched up in a fist,
   a diff'rent signal make;
   the threat of violence is clear,
   avoiding action take.

4. Hands waved aloft to greet
   someone returning home;
   they show just how they have been missed,
   while 'cross the world they roam.

5. Hands held up high to bless,
   cleansed sinners near and far;
   they brought the loving touch of God
   to those most would debar.

6. Hands held out on a cross,
   were once nailed to a tree;
   yet these were arms held out in love,
   to set the whole world free.

7. Hands of the risen one,
   marked with the scars of love,
   they hold the promise to us all
   that we can know such love.

8.     Hands come in many sorts
       and diff'rent colours too;
       it's what they do that matters most,
       and how that love shines through.

**TUNE: 66.86. S.M.**                    **Gildas (St. Augustine)**
From a plainsong melody
adapted from the chorale *Als de gutige Gott*
in J. S. Bach's *Vierstimmige Choralgesange* (1769)
[Hymns & Psalms 614]
[Singing the Faith 590]

**TUNE: 66.86. S.M.**                    **Potsdam**
Adapted from J. S. Bach (1685-1750)
[Hymns & Psalms 734]

## 22 I was lost and alone

1. I was lost and alone,
   bewildered, full of fear;
   my dreams and hopes a worthless stone,
   and no-one would come near.

2. Darkness was all around,
   no one could share my pain;
   lost and alone on shifting ground,
   there destined to remain.

3. Since then a light has come,
   transformed my wretched state;
   the way is clear, I've found a home,
   and I am feeling great.

4. Lord, you have rescued me,
   you've bathed me with your light;
   for you have calmed my troubled sea,
   now all my days are bright.

5. "Come unto me," you said.
   I heard you speak to me,
   "Come, walk with me, lift up your head
   and I will set you free."

6. So now I sing your praise,
   the praises of my Lord;
   through all my days my voice I'll raise,
   to praise God's living Word.

TUNE: 66.86. S.M.                    Carlisle
C. Lockhart (1745-1815)
[Hymns & Psalms 513(i)]
[Singing the Faith 370(ii)]

## 23 Waiting, waiting, waiting
### Jesus the healer

1. Waiting, waiting, waiting, waiting for the day,
   waiting to meet Jesus, passing down this way.
   When will he come, I'm sure he'll come this way,
   I am waiting now, O will he come today?

2. Poor blind Bartimaeus, waiting by the road,
   just a poor blind beggar, contempt people showed.
   When Jesus came, he made the blind man see,
   then he followed Jesus, who had set him free.

3. At the pool, Siloam, sick and needy pray,
   in its troubled waters hoped their healing lay.
   When Jesus came, he stopped where the man lay,
   'Now get up I tell you', made him well that day.

4. Frenzy in a graveyard, Legion on the loose,
   ev'ryone was fearful of this strong recluse.
   When Jesus came he freed him from abuse
   demons made an offer they could not refuse.

5. Waiting, waiting, waiting, waiting for the day,
   waiting to meet Jesus, passing down this way.
   When Jesus comes, I know he'll come this way;
   I am waiting for him, here he comes today.

TUNE: 11.11.10.11.          Noel Novelet
French Melody
Arranged by Geoffrey Laycock (1927-86)
[Hymns & Psalms 204]
[Singing the Faith 251 / 306 / 524]

## 24 Lord, we come to tell the story
**Testimony**

1. Lord, we come to tell the story,
   celebrate what you have done;
   Yours alone the praise and glory,
   Christ, the true, the only One.

2. Here you welcome all who gather,
   those baptised into your Name;
   Called, empowered, yours forever
   through the Spirit's burning flame.

3. Some you call to preach the Gospel,
   some ordained to break the bread;
   Others called to serve the people,
   all will follow in your stead.

4. Lord, you call us all to service
   all who bear the cross of Christ;
   Through our actions may we witness
   to the one who paid love's price.

5. Lord, you take our story onwards,
   on the yet unwritten page;
   In the Spirit lead us forward,
   we will serve you in each age.

6. So, Lord, may we tell the story,
   celebrate what you have done;
   Yours alone the praise and glory,
   Christ, the true, the only One.

TUNE: 8.7.8.7.                    **Servant Song**
Richard A. M. Gillard (b.1953)
Arranged by Betty Pulkingham (b.1928)
[Hymns Old & New 91]
[Singing the Faith 611]
[Hymns Old & New Revised 91]

# 25 Jesus Christ, incarnate Lord

1.  Jesus Christ, incarnate Lord,
    born among us, God's true Word;
    travel with us day by day,
    as we walk the Christian way.
    Jesus, Friend and Brother true,
    may we walk this way with you.

2.  Jesus Christ, nailed to a cross,
    who can quantify such loss?
    Yet you triumphed on the tree,
    pain and death to set us free.
    Jesus, how such love as this
    was betrayed by just one kiss.

3.  Jesus Christ, the risen Lord,
    what a message we have heard;
    we're the ones who have not seen,
    we believe the Nazarene.
    Jesus, Easter's life anew
    fill us as we follow you.

4.  Jesus Christ, ascended high
    to the place where none can fly;
    in God's presence, day by day,
    bless us, Lord, for that we pray.
    Jesus, high exalted Lord,
    bless us through your living Word.

5.  Jesus Christ, the Spirit true
    came to work through all we do;
    sharing gifts and graces too,
    may we live to honour you?
    Jesus, promised us that we
    all his work of love would see.

6.  Jesus Christ, in Church and world,
    see love's banner is unfurled;
    guide your people as they live,
    using all they have to give.
    Jesus, Lord, we offer you
    all that love and faith can do.

**TUNE: 77.77.77.**                    **Noricum**
**Frederick James (1858-1922)**
**[Hymns & Psalms 791]**
**[Singing the Faith 102(ii)]**

## 26 No Jew or Gentile, slave or free
### One in Christ – Galatians 3:28

1. Not Jew or Gentile, slave or free,
   not male nor female, black or white,
   for in Christ Jesus all are one,
   and all are equal in God's sight.

2. A love that welcomes one and all,
   the all-inclusive love of God;
   Christ calls his servants now his friends,
   he is God's true and living Word.

3. See him stretched out upon a cross,
   nailed to the tree by human hands;
   the Christ who hangs there pleads for all
   in Jewish or in Gentile lands.

4. Three things describe the love he shows,
   a love of God and neighbour too;
   the love Christ shows has a third part:
   the love of self, of me and you,

5. The love of God, it knows no bounds,
   it reaches all the human race;
   for in Christ Jesus all are one,
   one family in time and space.

6. No race, or culture, gender, creed,
   can separate us from this love;
   for in Christ Jesus all coheres,
   life here on earth and life above.

7. So join your hands and voices too,
   sisters and brothers of the Lord;
   through Easter Christ has made you one,
   now live the message you have heard.

TUNE: 88.88. L.M.          Niagara
Robert Jackson (1840-1914)
[Hymns & Psalms 619(i)]
[Singing the Faith 596]
[Hymns Old & New Revised 464]
[Mission Praise Combined 656(ii)]

## 27  In Christ alone, I travel on
**A disciple's prayer**

1.  In Christ alone, I travel on,
    he is my Saviour, Lord and Friend;
    he walks with me, he teaches me
    the wonders of love without end.
    We travel on down life's highway,
    each bound together day by day;
    He is my Lord, I am his friend,
    each bound to each, love without end.

2.  With Christ alone, I'll live each day,
    love God and neighbour is his way;
    all that I hope and strive to be,
    clothed in his love, for this I pray.
    A new command for me and you,
    to love ourselves and others too;
    He is my Lord, I am his friend,
    through bonds of love that have no end.

3.  Through Christ alone, the way ahead
    it will be hard, the journey long;
    yet with the Lord, I'll courage take,
    this is my life, my way, my song.
    My cross I'll take, this is the price,
    his praises rise through sacrifice;
    He is my Lord, I am his friend,
    we'll travel on to journey's end.

4.  In Christ alone, I'll rise one day,
    to share eternity with him;
    he is the one, the Easter Christ,
    once crucified, sin's pure victim.
    The Lord of earth, the King of heav'n,
    the one through whom I am forgiv'n;
    He is my Lord, I am his friend,
    still bound as one, life without end.

TUNE: 8.8.8.8.8.8.8.8.8                    **In Christ alone**
**Keith Getty (b.1974) and Stuart Townend (b.1963)**
**[Hymns Old & New Revised 352]**
**[Singing the Faith 351]**

# 28 Carpenter from Nazareth

1. Carpenter from Nazareth –
   wield your tools of saw and plane;
   Men and women find new birth –
   honed and shaped in your domain.

   *Knock! Knock! Knock!*
   *You hone and shape the wood.*
   *Tap! Tap! Tap!*
   *You're making something good.*
   *Take and mould us.*
   *Mould and shape us.*
   *That we may be all we should.*

2. Carpenter from Nazareth –
   hew the sculpture from the wood;
   Shape of heaven on the earth –
   mould your pattern for our good.

3. Carpenter from Nazareth –
   chisel out the shape you see;
   Making people of great worth –
   kingdom workers we will be.

4. Carpenter from Nazareth –
   plane the rough to make it smooth;
   Let the Kingdom come to birth –
   in your servants here on earth.

5. Carpenter from Nazareth –
   seeking joiners every day;
   Guide your people on this earth –
   lead them in the Kingdom way.

TUNE: 7.7.7.7. and refrain Children's Praise
Curwen's Tune Book (1842)
[Hymns & Psalms 163]
[Mission Praise Combined 70]

# Advent

# 29 Through Advent let us pause a while

1.  Through Advent let us pause awhile
    amid the Winter spending spree;
    a rest within the busy rush
    to gather all we want or see.
    To hear again the still small voice
    that points us to the Kingdom choice.

2.  For Advent tells of promises,
    made to a people long ago;
    how through the fearless prophet's word
    the Word of God they came to know.
    Like them we hear the still small voice
    that points us to the Kingdom choice.

3.  In Advent comes a strident voice
    out in the desert places heard;
    for John the Baptist cries to all,
    "Prepare yourself!" – a piercing word.
    And still we hear the still small voice
    that points us to the Kingdom choice.

4.  Through Advent choices must be made,
    and lowly Mary made hers too;
    for God himself was to be born,
    the Word made flesh in human view.
    With her we hear the still small voice
    that points us to the Kingdom choice.

5.  So Advent days are precious still,
    as we prepare for Christmas-time,
    they help us to recall again
    the meaning of this special time.
    To hear again the still small voice
    that points us to the Kingdom choice.

**TUNE: 88.88.88.**                    **Abingdon**
Eric Routley (1917-82)
[Hymns & Psalms 500]
[Singing the Faith 359 / 499]
[Hymns Old 7 New Revised 270]

# 30 Watching and Waiting

1. Watching and waiting, time is drawing near,
   Waiting and watching, he will soon appear;
   Watching and waiting, looking for the Lord,
   We wait and watch until his voice is heard.

2. Lord we are waiting for the promised time,
   When voices to one tuneful song will rhyme;
   And all who greet your great and glorious day
   Will walk with joy along your holy way.

3. We watch until the time when he draws near,
   The holy One from God among us here;
   Who in the midst of human life will call
   And speak the words of God to each and all.

4. We watch with patience for your coming, Lord,
   We read the words your promises record;
   We hear again the voice that must be heard,
   It speaks out from your true and lively Word.

5. So now we're waiting in these Advent days,
   Still searching out your holy will and ways;
   Waiting and watching, as the time draws near,
   We watch and wait to make you welcome here.

6. Let all the bells ring out across the earth,
   To tell the news about the coming birth;
   When those of faith who watch and wait will see
   The Christ at whose Name all will bow the knee.

TUNE: 10.10.10.10.          Woodlands
Walter Greatorex (1877-1949)
[Hymns & Psalms 86]
[Singing the Faith 186]
[Mission Praise Combined 631(ii)]

# 31 Advent candle shining bright

## Week One

1. Advent candle shining bright
   we can see your dancing light ;
   God's great plan is coming true,
   his pure light is shining through.
   Sing the Advent song.

## Week Two

2. Long ago in ancient time
   prophets voiced their Godly rhyme;
   God's clear light and message true
   pierced the darkness, just like you.
   Sing the Advent song.

## Week Three

3. Cousin John began his work –
   the Baptiser did not shirk;
   Called the people to draw near –
   herald of God's Son is here.
   Sing the Advent song.

## Week Four

4. Maiden Mary had a fright –
   Angel's message in the night;
   She said 'yes' to God's great plan –
   through her womb God comes a man.
   Sing the Advent song.

## All Weeks

5. God's light shines bright on the earth,
   pointing to the Saviour's birth;
   Let us walk the Advent road,
   soon his story will be told.
   Sing the Advent song.

TUNE: ORIENTIS PARTIBUS 77.77.5
Medieval French Melody arr. Ralph Vaughan Williams (1872-1958)
[Hymns & Psalms 168]
[Singing the Faith 326]

*Advent One:* *Verse 1 + 5*
*Advent Two:* *Verse 1 & 2 + 5*
*Advent Three:* *Verse 1,2 & 3 + 5*
*Advent Four:* *All verses*

## 32 On Advent Sunday number one

1.    On Advent Sunday number one,
      we mark that all things have begun,
      that God in Christ is on the way
      and we prepare for his birthday.

2.    On Advent Sunday number two,
      the prophet's words of hope ring true,
      that God has promised to draw near,
      his Word in flesh will soon appear.

3.    On Advent Sunday number three,
      we hear the Baptist's urgent plea:
      'Prepare the way, make his path straight,
      hark the Lord comes to end your wait.'

4.    On Advent Sunday number four,
      the angel knocks on Mary's door,
      'You will be mother to God's Son.'
      Once she said 'Yes!' then it was done.

5.    In Advent let the Church prepare
      to welcome Christ, his Name declare,
      to sing with joy through Advent days
      and fill his coming with God's praise.

6.    Prepare yourselves through Advent days,
      to greet the Lord who comes with praise;
      let all who bear his blessed Name,
      prepare yourselves, God's love proclaim.

TUNE: 88.88. L.M.          **Tallis' Canon**
**Melody and most of the harmony by Thomas Tallis (c.1505-1585)**
**Ravencroft's** *Psalmes*, **1621**
**[Hymns & Psalms 765]**
**[Singing the Faith 142]**
**[Mission Praise Combined 176]**

*Advent One: Verse 1 + 5 & 6*
*Advent Two: Verse 1 & 2 + 5 & 6*
*Advent Three:          Verse 1,2 & 3 + 5 & 6*
*Advent Four:           All verses*

# 33  When the voice of God was drowned
**The Prophets**

1.  When the voice of God was drowned
    in the Hebrew people's past;
    By the splendour of the king
    and in things that did not last;
    So God chose a prophet's voice
    to set out his people's choice.

2.  When the ways of God were spurned
    by the leaders of man-kind;
    Or by skill of human art
    and the musings of the mind;
    Then the prophet's voice was heard
    speaking God's persistent word.

3.  So the call for righteousness
    and for justice, truth and peace,
    Call earth's stewards to account,
    demand war's mad clamour cease;
    Speak God's calm and loving choice
    through the brave prophetic voice.

4.  Still the prophet speaks today
    pointing to both need and hurt;
    Speaking out the forceful word
    and with courage truth assert;
    Hear the wisdom of their word,
    let the prophet's voice be heard.

5.  So God's ways still earn their place
    in the midst of human life;
    Working hard against the tide,
    speaking peace amid the strife;
    Hear again the still small voice
    prophets offering God's choice.

TUNE: 7.7.7.7.7.7.                    Dix
C. Kocher (1786-1872)
Adapted by W. H. Monk (1823-89)
[Hymns & Psalms 121]
[Singing the Faith 224]
[Hymns Old & New Revised 46 / 196]
[Mission Praise Combined 39]

# 34 Prophets come in many guises
**The Prophets**

1. Prophets come in many guises:
   artists and the activists,
   poets, priests and music makers,
   doctors, teachers, scientists,
   So they challenge all our thoughts and ways
   for the Lord of all our days.

2. Prophets call us to account here,
   for the way we use the earth;
   as the problems mount around us,
   threatening both life and birth;
   So they challenge all our thoughts and ways
   for the Lord of all our days.

3. Prophets see our ravaged planet,
   call on us to take more care.
   battered earth, swamped in pollution,
   waste and rubbish ev'rywhere;
   So they challenge all our thoughts and ways
   for the Lord of all our days.

4. Prophets see the needs of people,
   bring their plight before our eyes;
   those still starving or neglected,
   open our ears to their cries;
   So they challenge all our thoughts and ways
   for the Lord of all our days.

5. Prophets speak your words of wisdom,
   point us to the way ahead;
   change the aims of self-delusion,
   teach us how to care instead;
   So they challenge all our thoughts and ways
   for the Lord of all our days.

TUNE: 8.7.8.7.8.7.                    **Picardy**
French Carol Melody as harmonised in The English Hymnal (1906)
[Hymns & Psalms 266]
[Singing the Faith 591]
[Hymns Old & New Revised 424]

# 35  The Baptist cried on Jordan's bank
### John the Baptist

1. The Baptist cried on Jordan's bank:
   'Behold the Christ draws near.
   Prepare yourselves to meet with him
   for he will soon appear.'

2. The people came from near and far,
   responding to John's word.
   'Turn round and seek the way of God,'
   he told the eager crowd.

3. Among the thousands Jesus came
   to be baptised by John.
   Then when the Father spoke to him,
   Jesus, God's work began.

4. Jesus called twelve, his special friends;
   he taught and preached and healed,
   And on the Cross at Calvary
   the love of God revealed.

5. Lord God, in Advent we prepare:
   we hear the Baptist's call.
   We hail and recognise your Son,
   Saviour and Lord of all.

**TUNE: CM**                              **St. Columba**
**Petrie** *Collection of Irish Melody* **harmonised Compilers of Irish** *Church*
***Hymnal.* 1874**
**[Hymns & Psalms 469(ii)]**
**[Singing the Faith 680 / 712]**

# 36 To lowly Mary, young and fair
Mary

1. To lowly Mary, young and fair,
   the angel message caused a stir.
   God's chosen mother for his Son,
   unmarried and so very young.
   *O lowly Mary, lead us too,*
   *along God's holy way with you.*

2. So humble Mary, unafraid,
   said: 'Yes' to God's angelic word.
   God's chosen mother for his Son
   said: 'Yes', and lo the deed was done!
   *O humble Mary, lead us too,*
   *along God's holy way with you.*

3. For gentle Mary, trav'lling far
   from Nazareth to Beth'lem's star.
   God's chosen mother for his Son
   at Caesar's word she must go on.
   *O gentle Mary, lead us too,*
   *along God's holy way with you.*

4. To anxious Mary, nearing time,
   "No room! No room!" a heartless rhyme.
   God's chosen mother for his Son
   in stable bare she births the One!
   *O anxious Mary, lead us too,*
   *Along God's holy way with you.*

5.    For mother Mary, filled with joy,
      Jesus, her new-born baby boy.
      God's chosen mother for his Son:
      lowly and gentle, holy one.
      *O mother Mary, lead us too,*
      *Along God's holy way with you.*

TUNE: 88.88.88.                    Sussex Carol
English traditional melody collected and arranged by Ralph Vaughan Williams
(1872-1958)
[Hymns & Psalms 364]
[Singing the Faith 148 / 534]
[Mission Praise Combined 537]
[Hymns Old & New Revised 588]

It would be possible for a soloist or choir to sing the first part of each verse
with the congregation singing the refrain.

# 37 The waiting almost over

Mary

1. The waiting's almost over,
   the birthing time draws near,
   but where I'll have my baby
   is anything but clear.
   We're on the road to Judah,
   dear Joseph leads the way,
   but where I'll have my baby,
   we have no place to stay.

2. It all seems so long ago,
   the angel came to me,
   yet in my womb God's baby
   is ready to be free.
   I've trusted you so far, Lord,
   your words have all come true,
   so where I'll have my baby,
   I'll have to leave to you.

3. The couple travel onwards,
   to Bethlehem at night,
   for there she'll have her baby,
   before it is daylight.
   With Mary we prepare now,
   to greet her new-born son,
   for Christmas is upon us,
   we greet God's holy One.

TUNE: 7.6.7.6.D.                    Aurelia
Samuel Sebastian Wesley (1810-1876)
[Hymns & Psalms 515]
[Singing the Faith 690]
[Hymns Old & New Revised 645, 702]
[Mission Praise Combined 126, 640]

# 38   Come magnify the Lord with me
## Mary Magnificat  - Luke 1:46 - 55

1.     Come magnify the Lord with me,
my soul rejoices inwardly;
with favour he has looked on me,
his lowly servant he sets free.

2.     He loves all those who walk his way,
down through the ages and today;
his strength is known when needs are great
but all the proud find they must wait.

3.     The mighty he brings down to earth,
exposing all their false self worth;
the poor and needy lifted high,
the rich brought low, the needle's eye.

4.     He fills the hungry with good things
and to his Name their praise they sing;
the rich are full of this world's things,
they praise themselves, that's all they bring.

5.     His promises will all come true,
his mercy he remembers too;
and Israel he won't forget,
on Abram's children love is set.

6.     Now we are blessed, for God is good,
we trust God's loving parenthood.
And soon the whole wide world will know
for all God greatness we will show.

TUNE: 88.88. L.M.          Herongate
Traditional English melody collected and arranged by
Ralph Vaughan Williams (1872-1958)
[Hymns & Psalms 844]
[Singing the Faith 415, 659]
[Hymns Old & New Revised 364]

# 39 Orange round and blood-red ribbon

**A Christingle celebration**

1. Orange round and blood-red ribbon,
   Lighted candle, fruits to share;
   Let Christingle tell the story
   through these symbols of God's care.

2. So Christingle tells a story
   of a world of pain and greed;
   Blue and beautiful in space, yet
   crying out in hope and need.

3. The Christingle tells the story
   of the coming of God's light;
   Born a baby in a stable,
   light that shines in darkest night.

4. The Christingle tells the story
   of salvation for the world;
   Love of God that knows no limit,
   love's red ribbon is unfurled.

5. The Christingle tells the story
   of the growing fruits of love;
   Spirit's power on each bestowing,
   works of grace through fire and dove.

6. The Christingle tells our story
   of a people saved through grace;
   Through this symbol and our singing –
   know the warmth of God's embrace.

TUNE: 8.7.8.7.       Laus Deo [Redhead 46]
Richard Redhead (1820-1901) from Church Hymn Tunes (1853)
[Hymns & Psalms 445]
[Hymns Old & New Revised 88]

# 40 So dark against the light you stand
## Festival of the Chrismon Tree

1. So dark against the light you stand,
   Your branches stark and bare;
   The evergreen tells ev'ry land
   God's love is always there.

2. The tiny lights upon our tree
   Tell of your light, O Lord;
   The star that brought those Wise Men three,
   To seek you from abroad.

3. The cross stands at the very heart,
   Christ died on our behalf;
   These shapes and patterns of our art
   Point to his saving life.

4. The lamb and fish and staff and dove,
   Angel and cup and flame;
   Our Chrismons pointing to your love,
   We glorify your Name.

5. The monograms upon our tree
   The story of Christ tell;
   The Lord who comes will set us free,
   He will make all things well.

6. We wait your coming gracious Lord,
   Into our Advent night;
   Come down upon us, living Word,
   And bathe us in your light.

TUNE: 8.6.8.6.                     Tallis' Ordinal
Melody and most of the harmony by Thomas Tallis (c. 1505-85) as in Ravencroft Psalmes, 1621
[Hymns & Psalms 586]
[Singing the Faith 392 / 538]
[Hymns Old & New Combined 554]

## 41 Advent days are here upon us
**Festival of the Chrismon Tree**

1.  Advent days are here upon us
    Christmas-time is almost here;
    Chrismon Tree – our celebration
    of the Christ who now draws near.
    *Christ our light,*
    *Shining bright,*
    *Help us all to share your light.*

2.  All the dark and spiky branches,
    Speak of life through evergreen;
    So the life of God eternal
    In his Son that gift was seen.
    *Christ our light,*
    *Shining bright,*
    *Help us all to share your light.*

3.  On the branches lights are shining,
    Pure and white as God's true light;
    For the world his light was given –
    Jesus said, 'I am the light.'
    *Christ our light,*
    *Shining bright,*
    *Help us all to share your light.*

4.  Symbols hanging on the branches,
    Shells and stars and crosses too;
    Monograms of Christ our Saviour
    Symbols of his life so true.
    *Christ our light,*
    *Shining bright,*
    *Help us all to share your light.*

5.   Lord, meet with us as we gather,
     We would be your Chrismons too;
     Lights along the pilgrim pathway,
     Yours in all we say or do.
     ***Christ our light,***
     ***Shining bright,***
     ***Help us all to share your light.***

**Tune: 87.87.337.**                        **Michael**
**Herbert Howells (1892-1983)**
**[Hymns & Psalms 63(ii)]**
**[Singing the Faith 455(i)]**
**[Hymns Old & New Revised 19]**
**[Mission Praise Combines 16]**

# Christmas Day

**42**   **Starlight shines across the earth**
Christmas Day – lighting the central white candle

**43**   **The shepherds had their angels**

**44**   **See the eastern light is shining**

**45**   **Come let the bells ring out**

**46**   **In a borrowed stable bare**

**47**   **Long ago angelic singing**

**48**   **O Lord, incarnate here on earth**

**49**   **He is Jesus**

**50**   **The Christ is born**

## 42  Starlight shines across the earth
### Christmas Day – lighting the central white candle

1. Starlight shines across the earth,
   pointing to the Saviour's birth;
   Now let Christmas-time unfold,
   his great story must be told.
   Sing the Christmas song.

2. Bethlehem, the census-town,
   with the multitudes has grown;
   In a stable stark and bare
   Christ is born while others stare.
   Sing the Christmas song.

3. Temple shepherds sleeping sound
   by the angel host were found,
   Hear 'news of the Saviour's birth,
   in a stable born on earth.'
   Sing the Christmas song.

4. Into Bethlehem they went,
   found the place where they were sent;
   There they saw the holy child,
   and the night's events retold.
   Sing the Christmas song.

5. So we join them in their praise,
   and with joy our voices raise;
   Welcome we the Christ-child small,
   he will bring great joy to all.
   Sing the Christmas song.

6. Greet we now our lowly King
   and with joy and gladness sing.
   As they went their news to tell,
   we will share Good News as well.
   Sing the Christmas song.

TUNE: ORIENTIS PARTIBUS 77.77.4.
Medieval French Melody arr. Ralph Vaughan Williams (1872-1958)
[Hymns & Psalms 168]
[Singing the Faith 326]

# 43  The shepherds had their angels

1. The shepherds had their angels,
   the Wise Men had their star;
   But what have we to take us,
   to Bethlehem afar?
   It is the Christmas story,
   your coming, Lord, to earth;
   The message 'God is with us' –
   the story of your birth.

2. We celebrate your coming
   in Christmas word and song;
   We hear the old, old story,
   and know that we belong.
   So, may we hear the message
   that Christ is born on earth?
   With angels, shepherds, Magi,
   we celebrate your birth.

3. For Christ was born of Mary,
   a manger was his throne;
   See God and man together
   in Christ, and Christ alone.
   For this is incarnation,
   the God who comes to dwell;
   The Lord, among his people,
   Good News that we must tell.

**TUNE: 7.6.7.6.D.**                    **Aurelia**
**Samuel Sebastian Wesley (1810-1876)**
**[Hymns & Psalms 515]**
**[Singing the Faith 690]**
**[Hymns Old & New Revised 645, 702]**
**[Mission Praise Combined 126, 640]**

## 44  See the eastern light is shining

1. See the eastern light is shining
   in the breaking light of dawn;
   Once upon a Christmas morning
   here on earth God's Son, was born.
   *Light that marked a new beginning,*
   *shone upon that Christmas morn.*

2. Mary, Joseph and the Christ-child,
   in a lowly stable bare;
   born among us, Jesus, God's child,
   sleeps while others watch and care.
   *Light that marked a new beginning,*
   *shone upon that Christmas morn.*

3. With the shepherds at the manger,
   here we kneel in homage too;
   Welcoming a homeless stranger,
   one who will make all things new.
   *Light that marked a new beginning,*
   *shone upon that Christmas morn.*

4. On this holy Christmas morning,
   Lord, our joyful praises bring;
   As we celebrate the coming
   of the Christ, his praise we sing.
   *Light that marks a new beginning,*
   *shines upon this Christmas morn.*

TUNE: 8.7.8.7.8.7.                         Picardy
French Carol Melody as harmonised in The English Hymnal (1906)
[Hymns & Psalms 266]
[Singing the Faith 591]
[Hymns Old & New Revised 424]

# 45  Come let the bells ring out

1.  Come let the bells ring out,
    for Mary's child is born;
    come tell the world this joyful news
    upon a Christmas morn.

2.  Come raise your voices high
    and sing of  Bethlehem;
    for there the Son of God was born,
    the flower of David's stem.

3.  Come celebrate and sing,
    Good News for all today;
    God's Word takes flesh in human form,
    in holy interplay.

4.  Come at this Christmastime,
    and celebrate with joy;
    for God is with us in his Son,
    this new-born baby boy.

5.  Come let the news ring out,
    so all the world can hear;
    for Christ is born in David's town,
    our message: "God is here".

**TUNE: 66.86. S.M.**　　　　**Dominica**
**H. S. Oakeley (1830-1903)**
**[Hymns & Psalms 280(i)]**

**TUNE: 66.86. S.M.**　　　　**Carlisle**
**C. Lockhart (1745-1815)**
**[Hymns & Psalms 513(i)]**
**[Singing the Faith 370(ii)]**
**[Hymns Old & New Revised 87, 676,775]**

# 46   In a borrowed stable bare

1.  In a borrowed stable bare,
    while the ox and asses stare,
    Mary's God-child comes to birth,
    God is born upon the earth,
    *Let the joyous news be told,*
    *of the wonders we behold.*

2.  Joseph gives their child his name,
    Jesus, the one we acclaim,
    with a manger for a bed,
    in that lowly cattle shed.
    *Let the joyous news be told,*
    *of the wonders we behold.*

3.  On the hillside in the night,
    shepherds see a wondrous sight,
    angels' speak of peace on earth,
    heralds of the Christ-child's birth.
    *Let the joyous news be told,*
    *of the wonders we behold.*

4.  To the stable they are drawn
    on that holy Christmas morn,
    there they kneel in joyful awe,
    then they tell of all they saw.
    *Let the joyous news be told,*
    *of the wonders we behold.*

5.  Praise, O praise the new-born King,
    with the shepherds homage bring,
    hear the angels' message too,
    'Peace on earth', is told anew.
    *Let the joyous news be told,*
    *of the wonders we behold.*

TUNE: 7.7.7.7.7.7.                    Dix
C. Kocher (1786-1872)
Adapted by W. H. Monk (1823-89)
[Hymns & Psalms 121]
[Singing the Faith 224]
[Hymns Old & New Revised 46 / 196]
[Mission Praise Combined 39]

# 47  Long ago angelic singing

1.  Long ago angelic singing,
    heralded a Christmas morn;
    to some lowly shepherds bringing
    news that Christ the Lord was born.
    *Join our voices in the singing,*
    *Christ is born, yes Christ is born,*
    *Word made flesh upon the earth!*

2.  On this joyous Christmas morning
    let us celebrate his birth,
    for the Christ who brings God's blessing,
    is born here upon the earth
    *Join our voices in the singing,*
    *Holy Child, we hymn your birth,*
    *Word made flesh upon the earth!*

3.  Join the angel host in singing,
    tell the world that Christ is here;
    with the shepherds homage bringing,
    to the Holy Child so dear.
    *Join our voices in the singing,*
    *Christ is here, yes Christ is here,*
    *Word made flesh upon the earth!*

4.  Holy Jesus, on this morning,
    all our praise and worship bring,
    here we celebrate the dawning
    of your star, with joy we sing.
    *Join our voices in the singing,*
    *Holy Child, our praise we bring,*
    *Word made flesh upon the earth!*

TUNE: 8.7.8.7.8.7.7.  Divinum Mysterium
Late form of a Plainsong Melody as given in *Piae Cantiones* (1582)
arranged by David Valentine Willcocks (b. 1919)
[Hymns & Psalms 79]
[Singing the Faith 181]

# 48 O Lord, incarnate here on earth

1. O Lord, incarnate here on earth,
   born as a child you came to birth;
   and you, both human and divine,
   became God's most audacious sign.

2. You come to us weak as a child,
   so innocent and undefiled;
   yet through your life our God we see,
   once mind and heart are both set free.

3. Lord God incarnate, you transcend
   all that we know and comprehend;
   in weakness and in strength you reign,
   known through the Christ, in love's domain.

4. The Word made flesh, incarnate Lord,
   Jesus, the Christ, God's living Word;
   come teach us how to live God's way,
   come walk with us throughout each day.

5. Come holy child and show us how
   we are to serve and follow now;
   teach us your human way to live
   and to see God through all love gives.

**TUNE: 88.88. L.M.**            **Calm**
**J. B. Dykes (1823-76)**
**[Hymns & Psalms 308(ii)]**

## 49　He is Jesus

1.　　Angel voice, a message clear,
　　　 'You will bear my child so dear.'
　　　 God has spoken, Mary heard,
　　　 She accepts the promised word.
　　　 Hear the News! This child will be my Son.
　　　 Hear the News! This child will be my Son.
　　　 Call him Jesus;
　　　 Call him Jesus;
　　　 Call him Jesus, holy One

2.　　Single, pregnant, Oh what shame!
　　　 Others merely cast the blame.
　　　 Gentle Mary, meek and mild
　　　 Carrying her unborn child.
　　　 Hear the News! While others cast the blame.
　　　 Hear the News! While others cast the blame.
　　　 He is Jesus!
　　　 He is Jesus!
　　　 He is Jesus, Holy One

3.　　Faithful Joseph, full of doubt,
　　　 Will he see his problem out?
　　　 He too hears the voice of God
　　　 When the angel speaks God's Word.
　　　 Hear the News! This child will be my Son.
　　　 Hear the News! This child will be my Son.
　　　 Call him Jesus!
　　　 Call him Jesus!
　　　 Call him Jesus, holy One

4.   In a stable dark and bare,
     While the cattle watch and stare,
     Mary's child comes to its birth –
     God is born upon the earth.
     Hear the News! The child of God's own love.
     Hear the News! The child of God's own love.
     He is Jesus!
     He is Jesus!
     He is Jesus, God's own Son.

5.   Praise to Jesus, born today.
     Praise him on this holy day.
     Full of Christmas joy we raise
     Hearts and voices to his praise.
     Hear the News! God with us on the earth.
     Hear the News! God with us on the earth.
     Name him Jesus!
     Name him Jesus!
     Name him Jesus, God's own Son.

**TUNE: 7.7.7.7. and refrain Children's Praise**
Curwen's Tune Book (1842)
[Hymns & Psalms 163]

# 50 The Christ is born

1. Great God, enthroned in light sublime
   beyond the reach of space and time;
   The maker of all things that are
   comes to this earth a baby.

   *Sing! Sing! The Christ is born*
   *upon this holy Christmas morn.*
   *Praise! Praise! Your voices raise*
   *to Jesus, son of Mary.*

2. The shepherds contemplate the sight
   angels singing in the night;
   Sent to Bethlehem, to find
   the Christ, the promised baby.

3. A humble stable, cold and bare,
   ox and ass just feed and stare;
   There lowly Mary brings to birth
   her son, the longed-for baby.

4. The shepherds gathered at the stall
   to see the child, Lord of all;
   And Wise Men following a star
   bring their gifts for this baby.

TUNE: 87.87.68.67.          Greensleaves
Traditional English melody arranged by John Stainer
[Mission Praise Combined 749]
[Hymns Old & New 812]

# Watchnight and New Year

**51    The old year has now run its course**
For a Watchnight service

**52    The New Year lies before us**
New Year

## 51 The old year has now run its course
### For a Watchnight service

1. The old year has now run its course,
   and slips away, its time no more;
   The things we did, or failed to do,
   all shipwrecked on a distant shore.
   For time and tide, they never wait,
   against them, there is no debate.

2. The New Year comes, a time unlived,
   its space, its prospects all unknown;
   A page on which to write new things,
   a path to chart, a way to own.
   You're present, Lord, in all we do,
   the God who is, through old or new.

3. We thank you, Lord, for what is past,
   help us to learn its lessons too;
   For those who do not heed the past,
   repeat mistakes in what they do.
   Teach us the things we need to learn,
   that your great truth we may discern.

4. So, Lord, we enter this New Year,
   incarnate in our world you are;
   You walk with us along the way,
   and you will be our guiding star.
   Lord, may we walk this way with you,
   as you are making all things new?

5. Lord, we would fill this year with praise,
   and seek your guidance through its days.
   Help us, your truth to mark and learn
   that we may walk in all your ways.
   Incarnate Lord, walk with us still,
   your life, your way, your truth instil.

TUNE: 88.88.88.                    Pater Omnium
Henry James Ernest Holmes (1852-1938)
[Hymns & Psalms 801]
[Singing the Faith 562 / 716]

## 52 The New Year lies before us

1.    The New Year lies before us
we meet to sing your praise;
we're gathered here together,
our hearts and voices raise.
We bring our gifts and graces,
our love and worship too;
to offer all we are, Lord,
hearts, minds and spirits true.

2.    In Christ we come together,
he calls us to his side;
In Christ we journey onward,
our love we cannot hide.
Just where this year will take us
will only become known,
as we walk in the Spirit,
God's Kairos time we own.

3.    So, Lord, in praise and worship,
we gather in your name;
Come, guide us on this journey,
your kingdom way proclaim.
We'll travel ever onwards,
all walking in your way;
each trusting all to you, Lord,
and hearing what you say.

4.    Lord, may we know your blessing
as each new step we take?
through things that are familiar,
yet new responses make.
All that is new before us,
guide our responses too;
through old and new together
we'll serve and worship you.

**TUNE: 7.6.7.6.D.**                    Thornbury
Basil Harwood (1859-1949)
[Hymns & Psalms 784]
[Singing the Faith 692]
[Hymns Old & New Revised 772, 854]
[Mission Praise Combined 705]

**TUNE: 7.6.7.6.D.**                    Wolvercote
W. H. Ferguson (1874-1950)
[Hymns & Psalms 704(i)]
[Singing the Faith 563(i)]
[Hymns Old & New Revised 556,605, 716]

Kairos is 'God's time' or kingdom time' whereas Chronos is 'clock time' that
can be measured.

# Epiphany

# 53 A bright star in the eastern skies

1. A bright star in the eastern skies,
   it points to where a new king lies;
   the Magi head for Bethlehem,
   their precious gifts they take with them.
   *Sing, sing, sing out with joy,*
   *your mind and heart and voice employ;*
   *praise, praise, to Mary's child,*
   *the God revealed in Jesus.*

2. The gift of gold is for a king,
   a gift to this new child they bring;
   a king to reign from David's throne,
   God in this child the world will own.
   *Sing, sing, sing out with joy,*
   *your mind and heart and voice employ;*
   *praise, praise, to Mary's child,*
   *the God revealed in Jesus.*

3. Their second gift is frankincense,
   the priestly gift of great expense;
   this child, a priest from God divine
   will turn earth's water into wine.
   *Sing, sing, sing out with joy,*
   *your mind and heart and voice employ;*
   *praise, praise, to Mary's child,*
   *the God revealed in Jesus.*

4. The third gift is the strangest one,
   a gift of myrrh for this new son;
   this child will save his people too,
   through sacrifice he'll make things new.
   *Sing, sing, sing out with joy,*
   *your mind and heart and voice employ;*
   *praise, praise, to Mary's child,*
   *the God revealed in Jesus.*

5.   We celebrate Epiphany,
     and gather here on bended knee;
     we worship Christ the new-born king
     And to his manger gifts we bring.
     *Sing, sing, sing out with joy,*
     *your mind and heart and voice employ; praise,*
     *praise, to Mary's child,*
     *the God revealed in Jesus.*

TUNE: 87.87.68.67.          Greensleaves
Traditional English melody arranged by John Stainer
[Mission Praise Combined  749]
[Hymns Old & New 812]

# 54 Wise men on a journey

1. Wise men on a journey,
   following a star,
   seeking out the Christ-child,
   travel from a far.

2. Magi travel onwards,
   following the star,
   find him in a manger,
   stable door ajar.

3. Wise men bring their presents,
   from their homes afar,
   offer them to Jesus,
   God's new rising star.

4. Gold and myrrh they bring him,
   with sweet frankincense,
   offered to the Christ-child,
   gifts without pretence.

5. As we gather with them,
   worship too we bring,
   love the gift we offer,
   joy and praise we sing.

6. For our star is Jesus,
   born at Christmas-time,
   and the star we follow,
   he is light sublime.

7. So, we journey onwards,
   follow Christ our Lord,
   walking in the footsteps
   of God's living Word.

TUNE: 65.65.          Glenfinlas
K. G. Finlay (1882-1974)
[Hymns & Psalms128(i)]
[Hymns Old & New Revised 284]

TUNE: 65.65.          Worship
H. Mann (1850-1929)
[Hymns & Psalms 128(ii)]

# Ash Wednesday

**55**     Ashes of sorrow, our guilt at failed trust

**56**     Ashes to ashes, dust to dust

# 55 Ashes of sorrow, our guilt at failed trust

1. Ashes of sorrow, our guilt at failed trust,
   high hopes and promises turned into dust;
   the mark of your Cross we wear on our brow,
   only your saving grace can help us now.

2. Ashes of envy, contempt we can't hide,
   the sins of self-righteousness and of pride;
   the mark of your Cross we wear on our brow,
   only your saving grace can help us now.

3. Ashes of failure, of faith and of will,
   tasks undertaken and yet not fulfilled;
   the mark of your Cross we wear on our brow,
   only your saving grace can help us now.

4. Ashes we wear now, the sign of our sin,
   from our repentance let new life begin;
   the mark of your Cross we wear on our brow,
   only your saving grace can show us how.

TUNE: 10.10.10.10.          Morecambe
Frederic Cook Atkinson (1841-96)
[Hymns & Psalms 778]
[Mission Praise Combined 470]

# 56 Ashes to ashes, dust to dust

1.  Ashes to ashes, dust to dust,
    Such is our mortal frame;
    Sorrow and sadness turned to joy,
    Through love's eternal Name.

2.  Ashes of hopes once entertained,
    Lost in sins misty haze;
    Love and forgiveness bring to life
    Our past and future ways.

3.  Ashes of long-remembered sins,
    We now confess to you;
    Pour on the oil of blessedness,
    Restore what we once knew.

4.  Ashes to ashes, love transforms
    All that sin would destroy;
    God comes in Christ to make us new,
    Sin is replaced by joy.

5.  Ashes of sorrow, mark of joy,
    Upon our brow we bear;
    The cross of ashes, sign of hope,
    A hope we gladly wear.

**TUNE: 86.86. CM**          **St. Hugh**
**Edward John Hopkins (1818-1901)**
**[Hymns & Psalms 717(ii)]**
**[Singing the Faith 650]**
**[Hymns Old & New Revised 462 / 478]**

**TUNE: 86.86. CM**          **Amazing Grace**
**Scottish traditional melody**
**Or Early American folk melody arranged by Richard Lloyd**
**[Hymns & Psalms 215]**
**[Singing the Faith 440]**
**[Hymns Old & New Revised 34]**
**[Mission Praise Combined 495]**

# Lent

# 57  A chosen people, long ago

1. A chosen people, long ago,
   walked on God's freedom way;
   Jesus, the Son, must now forego
   his ease, to choose God's way.

2. Their journey lasted forty years
   his one of forty days;
   Alone with all life's hopes and fears,
   with evil's tempting ways.

3. The barren landscape, stark and bare,
   offered no hiding place;
   Cold frosty moon, sun's heat and glare,
   the snare of sin's embrace.

4. Yet, Lord, you did not yield to all
   the tempter's wily ways;
   you remained true to God's great call
   then and throughout your days.

5. The desert testing proved you true,
   it showed the way you'd take;
   God's love would shine in all you'd do,
   nothing such love would break.

6. As Lent begins we thank you, Lord,
   you made this journey too;
   So as we travel on this road,
   We'll travel it with you.

7. For forty years or forty days,
   until this war is won;
   Still seeking out God's will and ways,
   the journey still goes on.

**TUNE: 86.86. CM**                    **Bishopthorpe**
**Melody and bass from *Select Portions of the Psalms***
**published by H. Gardner, c. 1786**
**[Hymns & Psalms 763(i)]**
**[Hymns Old & New Revised 350]**

## 58 From Jordan's waters you emerged

1. From Jordan's waters you emerged,
   to take the Gospel way;
   the Spirit came, the Father spoke,
   to mark you out that day.

2. The Spirit led you on again
   into the wilderness;
   Why should you turn these stones to bread
   with power you possess?

3. Up to the highest place you rose,
   the temple's very top;
   Why should you put God to the test,
   your fall from there to stop?

4. So many voices clamour round
   to bid you worship them;
   Why should you stoop to lesser god's
   with God's love to proclaim?

5. Up from the desert place you came,
   the Kingdom way now clear;
   a way of such self-sacrifice
   when God would be so near.

6. O holy Lord, we worship you
   and at your feet we pray;
   Walk with us through these Lenten days
   and lead us in love's way.

TUNE: 86.86. C.M.                    Byzantium
Melody in Twelve Psalm Tunes, 1780 by Thomas Jackson (1717-17810
[Hymns & Psalms 698]
[Singing the Faith 557]

There are many Common Metre tunes to choose from.

# 59  Jesus, you were tempted

1. Jesus, you were tempted forty nights and days;
   suffered in the desert evil's darkest ways.
   This was your struggle, throughout forty days;
   the voice of the tempter offered easy ways.

2. Jesus, you were tempted: 'turn these stones to bread'.
   find some easy answer, show your pow'r instead.
   But you resisted that persuasive voice;
   'Go now, do not tempt me with that simple choice.'

3. Jesus, you were offered pow'r to rule the earth;
   first enslave its people, bind them all from birth.
   But you refused, Lord, to dance evil's tune;
   chose the path to freedom – the cost would come soon.

4. Jesus, you were challenged: 'demonstrate your pow'r.'
   and test God's commitment to his Son and heir.
   Lord, you rejected spectacular signs;
   took the way of service, followed God's designs.

5. Jesus, we are tempted as we live each day;
   and we lack your courage, walking on life's way.
   Help us, Lord Jesus, in the things we do;
   help us shun temptation as we follow you.

6. Jesus, may the Spirit bring us strength, we pray;
   to resist the tempter as we live each day.
   Teach us your ways, Lord, help us battle through;
   with your light to live by, may we journey too.

TUNE: 11.11.10.11.          Noel Nouvelet
French Carol arranged by Geoffrey Laycock (1927-86)
[Hymns & Psalms 204]
[Singing the Faith 251 , 396, 524]
[Hymns Old & New Revised 382]

We used the tune Noel Nouvelet in worship on our Circuit Staff Retreat. I was
already thinking about a hymn for the first Sunday in Lent. The combination of
circumstances proved to be the inspiration for this hymn on the temptations
Jesus faced and which we face ourselves today.

# 60 Voices in the desert place

1. Voices in the desert place,
   words within the wilderness;
   Made the hard and Kingdom choice,
   that would heart and will possess.
   *Lord, you chose a narrow way,*
   *sure God's Kingdom to display.*

2. Stones were littered all around,
   bread to eat was hard to find;
   'Turn these stones into your bread,'
   tempting words ran through your mind.
   *Lord, you chose a narrow way,*
   *sure God's Kingdom to display.*

3. On the temple's highest point,
   did you really want to fly?
   'Jump down now, he'll bare you up,
   God will not let his son die.'
   *Lord, you chose a narrow way,*
   *sure God's Kingdom to display.*

4. All the kingdoms of the earth,
   there arrayed for all to see;
   'Worship self, all is for you,
   worship me, you'll get the key.'
   *Lord, you chose a narrow way,*
   *sure God's Kingdom to display.*

5.  Lord, we struggle eve'ryday,
    searching for the way you took;
    Help us, as we follow you,
    may we have your true outlook?
    *We would choose your Kingdom way,*
    *may we walk with you each day?*

TUNE: 7.7.7.7.7.7.                    Dix
C. Kocher (1786-1872)
Adapted by W. H. Monk (1823-89)
[Hymns & Psalms 121]
[Singing the Faith 224]
[Hymns Old & New Revised 46 / 196]
[Mission Praise Combined 39]

# 61 On his own in the desert

1. On his own in the desert,
   Jesus stands alone;
   hopes and fears, dreams and nightmares,
   will he God's way own?
   This way, that way?
   Today, one day?
   On his own in the desert,
   Jesus stands alone.

2. On his own in the desert,
   will he find the way?
   conflicts, trials, day and night,
   will he own God's way?
   This way, that way?
   Today, one day?
   On his own in the desert,
   will he find the way?

3. On his own in the desert,
   searching for the light;
   how the darkness prowls around,
   probing day and night.
   This way, that way?
   Today, one day?
   On his own in the desert,
   searching for the light;

4. On his own in the desert,
   Jesus finds the way;
   he rejects the tempter's ploys,
   chooses what God says.
   This way? That way?
   Only God's way.
   On his own in the desert,
   Jesus finds the way;

TUNE: 7.5.7.5.44.7.5.      **Spirit of the Living God**
**Unknown**
**Arranged by W. G. Hathaway**
**[Hymns & Psalms 295]**
**[Singing the Faith 395]**

# 62 Upon our Lenten journey

1. Upon our Lenten journey,
   we travel with the Lord;
   we share his isolation,
   his struggles with the Word.
   The challenge of the Tempter,
   of peers, of self, of pride;
   all draw us from the pathway,
   and make us check our stride.

2. Lord God, you are the focus,
   of all we do and say;
   through faith and hope and love we
   live out the words we pray.
   Lord, use this Lenten journey
   to shape, to cleanse, to heal;
   we come as your disciples,
   may each your nearness feel.

3. Through acts of self-denial,
   of neighbourly goodwill;
   through days of prayer and fasting,
   to fortify the will.
   Such acts for the disciple,
   help discipline the soul;
   we contemplate the Godhead
   through whom we are made whole.

**TUNE: 7.6.7.6.D.**           **Thornbury**
**Basil Harwood (1859-1949)**
**[Hymns & Psalms 784]**
**[Singing the Faith 692]**
**[Hymns Old & New Revised 772, 854]**
**[Mission Praise Combined 705]**

# 63 We thank you for all mothers, Lord
**Mothering Sunday**

1.    We thank you for all mothers, Lord,
their nurturing and care.
They struggle to give birth to us,
risk all our lives to bear.
With tender love encourage us
to breathe and live and grow.
For mothers and for fathers too,
our thankfulness we show.

2.    Born in a stable far from home,
with Joseph looking on;
Mother of Jesus, holy child,
you birth your precious one.
Throughout his life and painful death,
you loved him day by day;
Sharing his pain and suffering
as mothers do today

3.    The Church of God is mother too,
to those Christ calls to serve;
A place of nurture and of faith,
where people grow in love.
We come together, Mother Church,
this Mothering Sunday,
To celebrate God's gift of life
and thank him for this day.

4.   Lord, if you are life's Father,
     it's source and nature's morn;
     Then you must be our mother too,
     midwife to each one born.
     Yours is the breath of life we breathe;
     your gift of life we live;
     Mother and Father to us all,
     our praise and thanks we give.

**TUNE: D.C.M.**                    **Noel**
**English Traditional Melody adapted and extended by Arthur Sullivan (1842-1900)**
**[Hymns & Psalms 108]**
**[Singing the Faith 205]**
**[Hymns Old & New Revised 363]**
**[Mission Praise Combined 345]**

**TUNE: D.C.M.**              **The Flight of the Earls**
**Irish Air Harmonised by F. B. Westbrook**
**[Methodist Sunday School Hymnbook 178]**

**I wrote this on the 30th March 2000 – the day my mother died!**

# 64 Whips were used for punishment

1. Whips were used for punishment,
   when people had done wrong;
   Pilate sent you to be flogged,
   what had you done so wrong?
   You came, proclaimed a Kingdom
   to all who'd hear your word;
   But was that such a crime, Lord,
   to let your voice be heard?

2. The leaders did not welcome
   the Kingdom you proclaimed;
   A Kingdom where their powers
   would be by love constrained.
   With Pilate they colluded
   to have you put to death;
   He let the soldiers flog you,
   then sentenced you to death.

3. Your scourged and broken body,
   bore the marks of our shame;
   Your love was just rejected,
   by those to whom you came.
   Yet by those stripes so painful,
   the world's great ills were healed;
   For through such pain and suff'ring
   God's love for us was sealed.

**TUNE: 7.6.7.6.D.**                    **Thornbury**
**Basil Harwood (1859-1949)**
**[Hymns & Psalms 784]**
**[Singing the Faith 692]**
**[Hymns Old & New Revised 772, 854]**
**[Mission Praise Combined 705]**

# 65 See the Christ is lifted high
**Passion Sunday or Good Friday**

1. See the Christ is lifted high,
   there enthroned upon a cross;
   'God forgive them' is his cry
   love's appeal in such a loss.

2. There alone against the sky,
   love's redeeming work is done;
   on the cross, uplifted high,
   love's great victory is won.

3. What a cost, what price to pay,
   such love in self-sacrifice;
   Christ would go no other way,
   this the way and this the price.

4. With the cross before we'll go,
   followers of Christ the Lord;
   love's great banner we will show,
   witness to the saving Word.

5. Now the Christ is lifted high,
   on the cross is love's appeal;
   with him we will live and die,
   to such love our lives we seal.

TUNE: 77.77.        Song 13 (Canterbury)
Melody and bass by Orlando Gibbons (1583-1625)
[Hymns & Psalms 183]
[Singing the Faith 289]
[Hymns Old & New Revised 312, 367, 509]

# Palm Sunday

66  The noble beast of burden

67  He came astride a donkey

# 66 The noble beast of burden

1. The noble beast of burden
   steps out across the palms,
   The crowds they chant 'Hosanna'
   and cause some great alarms.
   The leaders from the Temple
   all scowl as you pass by,
   The children are excited –
   their loud 'Hosannas' cry.

2. The crowds press to the city,
   still causing quite a stir,
   The sounds of their 'Hosannas'
   like music fills the air.
   Some try to stop their praising,
   ask you to quell the throng,
   But still it grows the louder –
   a glorious triumph song!

3. They hail you 'Son of David',
   a king who comes in peace,
   The rulers call for silence,
   the music will not cease.
   Astride your beast of burden,
   the crowd acclaim you king,
   The leaders start their plotting –
   their evil omens bring.

4.    Lord, we would join their praises
      and greet you here today.
      We long to shout 'Hosanna'
      and crowd along your way.
      We'll mark your noisy entry
      into old Salem's streets,
      With palms and loud 'Hosannas'
      our Lord and Christ we greet.


**TUNE: 7.6.7.6.D**                    **Cruger (Herrnhut)**
From a melody by Johann Cruger's Gesangbuck (1640)
Adapted by W. H.Monk (1823-89)
[Hymns & Psalms 125]
[Singing the Faith 228]
[Hymns Old & New Revised 280]
[Mission Praise Combined 204]

## 67 He came astride a donkey

1.    He came astride a donkey,
the man from Galilee;
Down from the Mount of Olives,
the crowd were quick to see.
They raised shouts of 'Hosanna!' –
the crowds cut palms to wave;
They turned out in great numbers,
a joyous welcome gave.

2.    He came astride a donkey,
the people hailed their king;
His heralds in the prophets
told of the news he'd bring.
They raised shouts of 'Hosanna!' –
their cries rang in his ears;
'The blessed One among us,
God's kingdom must be near!'

3.    He came astride a donkey,
rode into Salem town;
Upon a beast of burden,
a king without a crown;
They raised shouts of 'Hosanna!' –
they came to greet their own;
He came in peace as promised
to claim his royal throne.

4.    We join our glad 'Hosannas!'
      to welcome you today;
      Our King, the Saviour Jesus,
      with all we sing and say.
      Hosanna to you, Jesus!
      Hosanna to the King!
      Hosanna to the Saviour!
      Hosanna, Lord, we sing!

**TUNE: 7.6.7.6.D.                          Cruger (Herrnhut)**
**From a melody by Johann Cruger's Gesangbuck (1640)**
**Adapted by W. H.Monk (1823-89)**
**[Hymns & Psalms 125]**
**[Singing the Faith 228]**
**[Hymns Old & New Revised 280]**
**[Mission Praise Combined 204]**

**It was strange to be in Egypt on Palm Sunday. About 10% of the population are Christian and there was an early morning procession to the Coptic Orthodox Church in Luxor with a donkey and palm branches. Unfortunately we weren't able to take part because of our 6.30am visit to the Valley of the Kings. But Irene, our Christian tour guide, obtained a Palm Cross for me. It was woven like a flat basket in the shape of a cross, with a bread cake in the pocket where the arms crossed.**

# Maundy Thursday

# 68 Who is this kneeling at my feet

**All**

1.    Who is this kneeling at my feet
with bowl and towel in his hand?
'Tis Jesus, who as servant kneels
ready to do the thing he planned.

2.    You must not wash my feet, dear Lord,
it's not a worthy job for you.
You are the greatest one I've known,
this thing I cannot let you do!

**Men only**

3.    You are not thinking as I think,
nor seeing things that I can see.
Let me wash you, make you all clean,
then you will all be one with me.

**All**

4.    Come, wash me, Lord, and make me clean,
so that I can be one with you.
You kneeling there was quite a shock –
a servant and my Saviour too!

**Women only**

5.    I have for you this pattern set,
to follow where your Master goes;
You are to live as servants too,
going the way the Master shows.

**All**

6.    Lord, you alone can make us clean
and lead us in God's living way;
Walk with us now, your servants too,
lead us throughout each livelong day.

**TUNE: 88.88.L.M.**          **Deep Harmony**
**Handel Parker (1854-1925)**
**[Hymns & Psalms 514(i)]**
**[Singing the Faith 90]**
**[Mission Praise Combined 620]**

**TUNE: 88.88.L.M.**          **Mainzer**
**Joseph Mainzer (1801-51)**
**[Hymns & Psalms 662]**
**[Singing the Faith 457]**

# 69 Jesus and the twelve

1. Jesus and the twelve were gathered,
   met in an upper room;
   Their Passover was all prepared,
   no hint of cross or tomb.

2. When Jesus knelt to wash their feet,
   the twelve were all surprised;
   'What I have done, you each must do.'
   They were all quite amazed.

3. Then while they ate he took some bread,
   broke it for all to share;
   'This is my body giv'n for you,
   pledge of my love and care.'

4. He took the cup and blessed the wine,
   the cup he bade them share;
   'This is my life I give for you,
   know I am always there.'

5. We meet you on this Maundy Night,
   we know your presence, Lord.
   You wash our feet and bid us dine,
   such is your gracious word.

6. We take these gifts as from your hands,
   met on this holy night;
   And we, invited to your feast,
   are guests by grace not right.

TUNE: 86.86. C.M.                    Bristol
Melody, and most of the harmony from T. Ravencroft's *Psalmes* (1621)
[Hymns & Psalms 82]
[Singing the Faith 171]
[Hymns Old & New Revised 288]

# 70 Jesus laid aside his garments

1. Jesus laid aside his garments,
   wrapped a towel round his waist;
   Then he took a bowl of water,
   knelt before each table guest.
   In the role of lowly servant,
   Jesus washed their dirty feet.
   Symbols of the bowl and towel,
   loving, leading, truly meet.

2. Looks of horror on their faces,
   Peter was indignant too;
   And when Jesus knelt before him,
   he resisted and argued.
   "Let me do this thing," said Jesus,
   "Let me show you what to do."
   Symbols of the bowl and towel,
   Jesus making all things new.

3. He accepted Jesu's offer,
   let the Teacher wash his feet;
   As we all did in amazement
   until Jesus took his seat.
   "Do you know what I have done here?
   You must wash each other's feet."
   Symbols of the bowl and towel,
   love's example to repeat.

4.    Bowl and towel and a servant,
Jesus points us to his way;
He has shown the great example,
love and leading interplay.
Servants not above their Master,
but must follow love's display.
Symbols of the bowl and towel
point us to Christ's unique way.

**TUNE: 87.87.D.**                  **Bethany**
**Henry Thomas Smart (1813-79)**
[Hymns & Psalms 653]
[Singing the Faith 25 / 110]
[Hymns Old & New Revised 241]

# 71 Your table is a place of truth

1. Your table is a place of truth,
   where friend and foe can meet;
   Betrayers and deniers too,
   your followers you greet.

2. But first you stoop to wash their feet,
   their Lord, a servant too;
   You show them how to lead and serve,
   teach them what they must do.

3. The truth lies there in bread and wine,
   foretaste of what will be;
   Your broken body, life-blood shed,
   the cup that sets us free.

4. In actions and in words you speak,
   the truth you have declared;
   The truth that is your sacrament,
   sign of your love and care.

5. Come meet us in your sacred meal,
   the Gospel truth engage;
   For we would serve you, Lord, today
   in this our time and age.

**TUNE: 86.86. C.M.**                    **Belmont**
**W. Gardiner's Sacred Melodies Volume 1 (1812)**
**Melody probably by William Gardiner (1770-1853)**
**[Hymns & Psalms 597]**
**[Singing the Faith 573]**

# Good Friday

# 72  There forsaken in the Garden

1.   There forsaken in the Garden,
     all his friends just ran away;
     One who came there to betray him,
     sealed his actions with a kiss.
     Lord, you stand alone, forsaken
     how have things all come to this?

2.   Jesus stands across the courtyard,
     chained and beaten and abused;
     Peter lingers there 'till morning
     and denied you at cock crow.
     Lord, you stand alone, rejected,
     how have things all turned out so?

3.   All the powers turn against you,
     Herod, Pilate, the High Priest;
     Must love bow its head to hatred,
     to such venom at the Feast?
     Lord, you bear the pain and sorrow,
     have your hopes and dreams now ceased?

4.   To the cross you stagger onwards,
     bowed beneath a heavy load;
     Cruel nails pin limbs and loving
     to the wood of Calv'ries' cross.
     Lord, you suffer for your loving
     has it all become a loss?

5.   Lord, we sing of love and sorrow
     that you bore upon the cross;
     Of the love that suffered for us,
     of the horror that we see.
     Lord, you carry all our failings,
     can such love now set us free?

6.  Lord, we sing on this Good Friday
    of your death upon the Cross;
    Love you made so real in living,
    now we see in pain and loss.
    Lord, in death your love transforms us,
    light and love shine from your Cross.

**TUNE: 8.7.8.7.8.7.**                    **Mannheim**
Melody adapted from a chorale in F. Filitz's *Choralbuch* (1847)
Harmony chiefly by Lowell Mason (1792-1872)
[Hymns & Psalms 68(i)]
[Singing the Faith 238]
[Hymns Old & New Revised 422]
[Mission Praise Combined 400]

# 73 High on a lonely hill

1. High on a lonely hill,
   the wounded healer cries;
   and now spread-eagled on a cross,
   forsaken, left, he dies.

2. He made the lame to run
   and made the blind to see;
   the lepers' scars were all made clean,
   he set the prisoners free.

3. The needy came to him,
   the deaf soon heard his name;
   he was the one who cared for all,
   he treated them the same.

4. See now he bears the scars,
   the very marks of love;
   he pays the price for such a gift
   that comes from God above.

5. His life now ebbs away,
   upon that cruel cross;
   is all that he has done in life
   now counted as his loss?

6.    Such love will never end,
      that claim is tested now;
      there on the cross he trusts it still
      we cannot fathom how.

7.    The wounded healer dies,
      his love for all unbowed;
      he trusts himself to God alone,
      not to the fickle crowd.

**TUNE: 66.86.S.M.**                         **Windermere**
**Arthur Somervell (1863-1937)**
**[Hymns & Psalms 589]**

**TUNE: 66.86.S.M.**                         **Franconia**
**William Henry Havergill (1793-1870) adapted from a tune in Konig's**
**Harmonischer Liederschatz (1738)**
**[Hymns & Psalms 585]**
**[Singing the Faith 244]**
**[Hymns Old & New Revised 78, 699]**

# 74 See blood-red flowers all adorn

1.    See blood-red flowers all adorn,
the vicious spines upon the thorn;
as once the drops of blood so red,
were smeared on thorns upon your head;
a crown of thorns they gave to you,
the humble king, the Lord Jesu.

2.    You bore the pain that seared your flesh,
love and self-sacrifice enmeshed;
and on the cross for them you prayed,
the ones who had your body flayed;
you bore all that they gave to you,
the servant king, the Lord Jesu.

3.    Then it was finished was your cry,
just one last word before you died;
your spirit gone, you hung your head,
still crowned with thorns, but you were dead;
they'd done their worst, they had killed you;
the lowly king, the Lord Jesu.

4.    Your body broken as you said,
there on the cross your blood was shed;
your friends were scattered in their fear,
only the woman all stayed near;
their hopes and fears all rest with you,
the noble king, the Lord Jesu.

5.    In faith we gather on this day,
the day that we call Good Friday;
the way of love you chose to go,
and on the cross such love you show;
now all our hopes we place in you,
our dying king, the Lord Jesu.

**TUNE: 88.88.88.**                    **Sussex Carol**
English traditional melody collected and arranged by Ralph Vaughan Williams (1872-1958)
[Hymns & Psalms 364]
[Singing the Faith 148 / 534]
[Hymns Old & New Revised 588]
[Mission Praise Combined 537]


**TUNE: 88.88.88.**                    **Abingdon**
Eric Routley (1917-82)
[Hymns & Psalms 500]
[Singing the Faith 359 / 499]
[Hymns Old 7 New Revised 270]


Anyone who has seen Mel Gibson's THE PASSION OF THE CHRIST will know what 'flayed' means!

# 75  In robes of royal purple hue

1.  In robes of royal purple hue,
    alone in Pilate's court you stand;
    The crowds know what they want to do,
    the Christ they reject out of hand;
    They want you hung upon the tree,
    but they are blind, they cannot see.

2.  Stark on the hill the three trees stand,
    their shadows fall across the earth;
    Hear! Hear! The crowds shout crucify!
    Their king rejected, of no worth.
    And Pilate, longing to be free,
    sends you to death upon the tree.

3.  So Pilate washes guilty hands,
    and has you flogged and scourged once more;
    Absolved, he sends you out to die,
    the Christ rejected by the law;
    The powers send you to the tree,
    and let a murderer go free.

4.  You bear the beam, the spar of death,
    the gloating crowds all line your way.
    They jeer and shout, you stagger by,
    the Christ rejected on that day.
    The Lord, who came to set them free,
    will die their death upon the tree.

5.  As you were raised upon the cross,
    those gathered round just stand and stare;
    They've had their way, you're crucified.
    Claim to be Christ, let all beware!
    Yet there, upon that painful tree,
    you die our death to set us free.

6.    Your cross stands stark against the sky,
      its shadow falls across the earth;
      We try to fathom why you died,
      a death that brought about new birth.
      O Lord, as you died on that tree,
      I know you bled and died for me.

**TUNE: 8.8.8.8.8.8.**                    **Melita**
**John Bacchus Dykes (1823-76)**
**[Hymns & Psalms 379]**
**[Singing the Faith 517]**
**[Hymns Old & New Revised 146, 160]**
**[Mission Praise Combined 122]**

# 76 Holy Week began so well

1. Holy Week began so well,
   Jesus in Jerusalem;
   things have changed and who can tell
   what's in store for him and them?

2. Judas sold him with a kiss,
   Peter claimed he didn't know;
   other friends were quite remiss,
   at his need such fear they show.

3. Pilate calmly washed his hands,
   priests and people bayed for blood;
   his disciples wrung their hands,
   on his own there Jesus stood.

4. Pilate sent him to the cross,
   priests and people got their way;
   all they gained was such a loss,
   Jesus would his God obey.

5. Stark against the greying sky,
   see the cross of Jesus stands;
   Man for Others, sent to die,
   crucified by cruel hands.

6. Now he lies, cold in the tomb,
   laid within a borrowed cave;
   sealed into a second womb,
   is love stronger than the grave?

TUNE: 77.77.                         Vienna
J. H. Knecht (1752-1817)
[Hymns & Psalms 764]
[Singing the Faith 676]
[Hymns Old & New Revised 80, 391]

# Easter Day

# 77  The sealing stone is rolled away

1. The sealing stone is rolled away,
   the grave clothes still where Jesus lay;
   The lifeless body is not there,
   where is the precious Master dear?
   **The Lord of cross and tomb is raised,**
   **now let the Easter Christ be praised.**

2. Peter and John race to the scene,
   with Mary see where he had been;
   They left perplexed but Mary stayed,
   she asked the gard'ner where Christ laid.
   **The Lord of cross and tomb is raised,**
   **now let the Easter Christ be praised.**

3. T'was Jesus and he spoke her name,
   dear Mary could not be the same;
   The herald of his rising, she
   worshipped her Lord on bended knee.
   **The Lord of cross and tomb is raised,**
   **now let the Easter Christ be praised.**

4. So full of joy her news proclaimed,
   but doubts the others entertained;
   'I've seen the Lord!' is what she said.
   'The Lord is risen from the dead!'
   **The Lord of cross and tomb is raised,**
   **now let the Easter Christ be praised.**

5.    With Alleluias sing your praise,
      God, Jesus from the tomb did raise.
      Come celebrate the Easter dawn
      with all who are in Christ reborn.
      **The Lord of cross and tomb is raised,**
      **now let the Easter Christ be praised.**

TUNE: 88.88.88.                        Abingdon
Eric Routley (1917-82)
[Hymns & Psalms 500]
[Singing the Faith 359 / 499]
[Hymns Old 7 New Revised 270]

I wrote this on Easter Sunday 2004 in Egypt at the El Gouna resort on the Red
Sea. We sang it together at our Easter Communion Celebration in the
apartment.

# 78  Lord, with praise we hail your glory

1. Lord, with praise we hail your glory
   On this resurrection morn;
   Joy and gladness tell the story,
   'Christ is raised, the world's new dawn!'
   Through the Cross, our God at Easter,
   Tragedy to Triumph turned.

2. At your tomb amazed disciples
   Struggled with perplexity;
   Lord, we echo their examples:
   Contemplate a mystery.
   Through the Cross, our God at Easter,
   Tragedy to Triumph turned.

3. Risen Lord, God vindicates you:
   Your Cross was the only way!
   Risen Lord, your Church acclaims you,
   Celebrates your Festal day!
   Through the Cross, our God at Easter,
   Tragedy to Triumph turned.

4. Praise to Jesus, Alleluia!
   Alleluia, risen Lord!
   Christ is risen, Alleluia!
   Alleluia, living Word!
   Through the Cross, our God at Easter,
   Tragedy to Triumph turned.

5. Lord and Christ, our risen Saviour,
   Fill us all with joy today;
   Sin and death, the great accuser,
   From our lives is driven away.
   Through the Cross, our God at Easter,
   Tragedy to triumph turned.

TUNE: 8.7.8.7.8.7.                    Grafton
French Church melody from Chants Ordinaires de l'Office Divin, Paris, 1881
arranged by Sydney Hugo Nicholson (1875-1947)
[Hymns & Psalms 402]
[Singing the Faith 696]

# 79  I'd tried to hide myself away
## Thomas's story

1. I'd tried to hide myself away,
   the day my Lord was crucified;
   To ponder on that fateful day,
   the day the Lord of life had died.

2. I'd tried to close my doubting ears,
   to the wild message of the ten;
   I would not hear the things they said,
   their claim that Jesus was risen.

3. I'd tried to shield my reeling mind:
   'I would believe what I could see';
   The risen Jesus came to find –
   the fearful and the doubting me.

4. I'd tried to shut my hopeless heart,
   but Jesus had come shining through;
   He sent us out to play our part –
   a people with his work to do.

5. I'd tried to find a way to cope –
   the risen Jesus came to me;
   Now doubting was replaced by hope
   for all through Christ have been set free.

TUNE: L.M. 88.88                    Duke Street
Melody, and most of the base, from H. Boyd's Psalm and Hymn Tunes (1793)
Later attributed to John L. Hatton (d. 1793)
[Hymns & Psalms 807]
[Singing the Faith 634}
[Hymns Old & New Revised 181, 200]
[Mission Praise Combined 143]

# 80 Two friends were walking home
## Road to Emmaus

1.  Two friends were walking home that day,
    Sharing their feelings on the way;
    As Jesus came and walked along,
    He knew they'd got things all quite wrong.
    "What are you talking of today?"
    He asked them as they went their way.

2.  They were surprised to find him there,
    A stranger who their journey shared.
    "The things back in Jerusalem!
    How could you not have heard of them?"
    All that the Scriptures had to say,
    He shared with them, their truth conveyed.

3.  And as they drew towards their home,
    They pressed the man to stay with them;
    He sat at table, took the bread,
    And as they heard the words he said,
    Their eyes were opened and they saw
    The Lord alive, with them once more.

4.  Then he was gone, they were alone,
    The risen Lord to them was known;
    They set off to Jerusalem
    To share the news given to them.
    "We saw the Lord," was what they said,
    "we knew him when he broke the bread."

5.  So as we gather here today,
    The Lord still travels down this way;
    Here at the table break the bread,
    For he is risen from the dead.
    He gives his gifts to all today,
    Who journey on the Christian way?

TUNE: 88.88.88.                    Pater Omnium
Henry J. E. Holmes (1852-1938)
[Hymns & Psalms 801]
[Singing the Faith 562 / 716]

# Ascension Day

81    Let us praise the Lord of heaven

# 81 Let us praise the Lord of heaven

1. Let us praise the Lord of Heaven,
   Throned beyond all time and space;
   Let us praise the Lord of Heaven,
   Saviour of the human race.
   ***Man who died,***
   ***Son who reigns:***
   ***Risen, ascended, glorified.***

2. Let us praise the Son incarnate,
   Jesus, Lord, our praise we bring;
   Let us praise the Son incarnate,
   Hymns and anthems loudly ring.
   ***Man who died...***

3. Let us praise our Christ ascended,
   Glorified in earth and heaven;
   Let us praise our Christ ascended,
   Songs of women and of men.
   ***Man who died...***

4. Let us praise our Lord and Saviour,
   From all peoples upon earth;
   Let us praise our Lord and Saviour,
   Praise his Name, proclaim his worth.
   ***Man who died...***

5. Let us praise the King in glory,
   Lord eternal, reigning now;
   Let us praise the King in glory,
   Every knee to him will bow.
   ***Man who died...***

TUNE: 87.87.337.              'Every Star'
A Shaker melody adapted by Sidney Carter (1915-2004) [Partners in Praise 46]

TUNE: 87.87.337.              Michael
Herbert Howells (1892-1983)
[Hymns & Psalms 63(ii)]
[Singing the Faith 455(i)]
[Hymns Old & New Revised 19]
[Mission Praise Combined 16]

# Pentecost

# 82 Holy Spirit, breath of God

1. Holy Spirit, breath of God,
   move within us while we pray;
   touch us with your fire of love,
   give us the right words to say.
   Holy Spirit, breath of God,
   move within us while we pray.

2. Holy Spirit, life of God,
   clothe our worship here today,
   breathe through all the words we sing,
   speak through Scripture words we say.
   Holy Spirit, life of God,
   clothe our worship here today.

3. Holy Spirit, love of God,
   gifts of fellowship display
   in our worship, through our life,
   and the things we do and say,
   Holy Spirit, love of God,
   gifts of fellowship display

4. Holy Spirit, light of God,
   shine upon us here today;
   come and fill this worship place,
   fill our lives from day to day.
   Holy Spirit, light of God,
   shine upon us here today.

**TUNE: 7.7.7.7.7.7.**         **Dix**
**C. Kocher (1786-1872)**
**Adapted by W. H. Monk (1823-89)**
**[Hymns & Psalms 121]**
**[Singing the Faith 224]**
**[Hymns Old & New Revised 46 / 196]**
**[Mission Praise Combined 39]**

# 83   In rushing wind and tongues of flame

1.   In rushing wind and tongues of flame,
     through hearts and minds set free;
     The signs the Spirit came with pow'r,
     and all could know and see.

2.   When silent voices rose to speak
     the truth that Jesus told;
     The Spirit surged within them all,
     no words could they withhold.

3.   And all could hear the message clear
     each in their native tongue;
     Their Babel turned to Pentecost,
     new life for old and young.

4.   The Spirit comes to us today,
     its gifts on each bestow;
     To raise us up to tell Good News
     that all through Christ shall know.

5.   The Spirit nerves our voice and song,
     the worship that we bring.
     In joyful praise we hail our God,
     of love and truth we'll sing.

**TUNE: 86.86. C. M.**          **Gerontius**
**John Bacchus Dykes (1823-1876)**
**[Hymns & Psalms 231(i)]**
**[Singing the Faith 334]**
**[Hymns Old & New Revised 627]**
**[Mission Praise Combined 563]**

**TUNE: 86.86. C. M.**          **Land of Rest**
**American Folk Hymn Tune**
**Harmonised by John Wilson**
**[Hymns & Psalms 621(i)]**
**[Singing the Faith 597]**

# 84  When chaos ruled, in power you came

1.  When chaos ruled, in power you came
    to still the forces of the night;
    the laws of order sure you frame
    and flood the universe with light.
    *Spirit of God, come fill our praise,*
    *as hearts and voices here we raise.*

2.  God's servants, prophet, priest and king,
    you summoned all: through still small voice,
    in mighty acts, and words that ring,
    revealed for all your kingdom choice.

3.  To Jordan river Jesus came,
    in water clear to be baptised;
    a dove of peace, you spoke his Name;
    Jesus, God's Son was recognised.

4.  The Spirit's power at Pentecost
    was on the Church of Christ bestowed;
    with gifts and graces all were blest -
    the Spirit through God's People flowed.

5.  O Holy Spirit, God of love,
    descend upon us here today;
    O may we to your music move,
    God's people in our work and play!

**TUNE: 88.88.88.**                    **Sussex Carol**
**English traditional melody collected and arranged by Ralph Vaughan Williams**
**(1872-1958)**
**[Hymns & Psalms 364]**
**[Singing the Faith 148 / 534]**
**[Hymns Old & New Revised 588]**
**[Mission Praise Combined 537]**

## 85 Spirit of God, in rushing wind

*Spirit of God, in rushing wind*
*And tongues of fire you came;*
*Touching the hearts of all in the room*
*Never to be the same.*

1.  Unless you lead,
    We stop and fail,
    We cannot know the Lord;
    Spirit of God,
    Come to our aid,
    Fulfil his promised word...

2.  Lead us, we pray,
    Your gifts bestow,
    As we live day by day;
    Send us to serve,
    Servants of Christ,
    Witnesses to his love...

3.  Spirit of love,
    Rule in our hearts,
    Teach us ways from above;
    Spirit of God,
    Show us the truth
    In Christ, the Living Word...

4.  Touch our hearts too,
    With God's own love,
    In all things make us new;
    Through love's great power,
    Teach us God's ways,
    Equip us for this hour...

*Spirit of God, in rushing wind*
*And tongues of fire you came;*
*Touch, Lord, the hearts of all in this room,*
*We'll never be the same!*

**TUNE: Irregular**           **Skye Boat Song**
**A Scottish folk melody**
**[Hymns Old & New Revised 213 / 697]**
**[Singing the Faith 394]**

# 86 Praise, O praise the Holy Spirit
**Based on Galatians 5:22-23**

1. Praise, O praise the Holy Spirit,
   bringing forth the fruit of love.
   Human lives display the fullness
   of the gifts of flame and dove.
   Holy Spirit, fount of grace,
   come and help us live in love.

2. First comes joy, with peace to follow –
   joy at God's great graciousness;
   peace the gift that Jesus promised;
   joy and peace bring blessedness.
   Holy Spirit, fount of grace,
   help us grow in holiness.

3. Kindness shows itself in service –
   loving people should be kind;
   patience grows in loving people
   as they realise God's mind.
   Holy Spirit, fount of grace,
   help us to be good and kind.

4. God of love, the faithful Spirit,
   always gracious, always true;
   faithfulness inspire within us –
   in our thoughts, in all we do.
   Holy Spirit, fount of grace,
   make us faithful, make us true.

5.   Holy Spirit, love embodied –
     gentleness is your gift too;
     self-control emerges slowly –
     touches everything we do.
     Holy Spirit, fount of grace,
     let us always live in you.


**TUNE: 87.87.77.**            **All Saints**
Adapted by W. H. Monk (1828-89) from a melody in *Geistreiches Gesangbuch*
(Darmstadt 1698)
[Hymns & Psalms 149(i)]
[Singing the Faith 725]
[Hymns Old & New Revised 828]

# 87 Breath of God, life of the Spirit

1.  Breath of God, life of the Spirit
    resting on all in this place;
    Gift of God, that Jesus promised,
    God's forgiving grace.

2.  Breath of God, come and renew us –
    gracious sign of love and power;
    Gift of God, that Jesus promised,
    everyone empower.

3.  Breath of God, the Holy Spirit
    poured into our hearts and lives;
    Gift of God, that Jesus promised,
    faith and hope revives.

4.  Breath of God, at work within us
    bringing forth your gifts of grace.
    Gift of God, that Jesus promised,
    to the human race.

5.  Breath of God, your work continue
    bringing forth the fruit of love.
    Gift of God, that Jesus promised,
    wind and fire and dove.

**TUNE: 8.7.8.5.**                    **St Leonard's (Gould)**
**Arthur Cyril Barham-Gould (1891-1953)**
**[Hymns & Psalms 739(ii)]**
**[Singing the Faith 504]**
**[Hymns Old & New Revised 506]**
**[Mission Praise Combined 463]**

## 88  The driving wind, across our face

1. The driving wind, across our face,
   just blowing where it wills;
   Power of the Spirit blowing too
   our empty lives it fills.

2. The burning fire, both hot and bright,
   consuming all the dross.
   Spirit of truth, like searing heat,
   come point us to the cross.

3. The tongues of earth communicate
   the words we use and speak;
   The tongues that with the Spirit came
   were heard by all who seek.

4. O gentle dove, your flight we see,
   across the land you wing;
   Dove of the Spirit now descend
   God's gifts of love to bring.

5. O Holy Spirit come to us
   in wind and fire and dove;
   Come fill us with the life you bring
   that we may show God's love.

TUNE: 86.86. C.M.   St.Botolph [Slater]
Gordon Archibold Slater (1896-1979)
[Hymns & Psalms 610(i)]
[Singing the Faith 588]
[Hymns Old & New Revised 194, 328]

# 89  As wind that sweeps across the sea

1.  As wind that sweeps across the sea,
    and blows throughout the land;
    Disturbing our tranquillity,
    the Spirit shows God's hand;
    Wind of the Spirit in us blow,
    that we God's Name may know.

2.  As fire that burns and yet refines,
    consuming, searing flame;
    The burning Spirit's power combines
    our love with your great Name;
    O burning Spirit show us how,
    that we may serve God now!

3.  As breath within us animates
    our mortal, human frame;
    The Spirit's breath in us creates
    the servants of the Name;
    Come breathe within us holy One,
    give life to everyone.

4.  As human beings learn to live
    and life's great blessings know;
    The living Spirit comes to give,
    God's blessings to bestow;
    Come Holy Spirit meet us now,
    let God's great blessings flow!

5.  As human voices sing and speak,
    in words of joy and praise;
    So God the Spirit comes to seek
    helpers in words and ways;
    Come speak your wisdom holy One,
    So may God's will be done.

TUNE: 8.6.8.6.8.6.          **Sheltered Dale**
**A German Traditional Melody**
**[Hymns & Psalms 631]**

129

# 90 The Spirit came upon the twelve

1. The Spirit came upon the twelve,
   all gathered in the upper room;
   they were a timid, frightened lot,
   and waiting with mixed hope and gloom.

2. The Spirit came upon the twelve,
   the breath of God, in wind and flame;
   their fears and doubts were soon consumed,
   they had the power to proclaim.

3. The Spirit came upon the twelve
   and brought the Church of Christ to birth;
   soon they were telling of the Name,
   prepared to go throughout the earth.

4. The Spirit came upon the twelve,
   they went into the market square;
   and people from the then-known world,
   heard in their tongues what they declared.

5. The Spirit comes upon us all,
   the Jesus people of today;
   Christ's promise is still coming true
   among his people here today.

**TUNE: 88.88. L.M.   Church Triumphant**
James William Elliott (1833-1915)
[Hymns & Psalms 182(ii)]

**TUNE: 88.88. L.M.                Bow Brickhill**
Sydney H. Nicholson (1875-1947)
[Hymns and Songs 14]
[Hymns & Psalms 182 (i)]
[Hymns Old & New Revised 804]

Every Easter Sunday at Sunrise we met for an early morning Communion on
Bow Brickhill 1981-1991 while we were in the Milton Keynes Circuit.
It became an ecumenical occasion with 150+ gathered together in a circle
much to the concern of the local constabulary!

I wrote this hymn on Wesley Day 2007.

# Trinity Sunday

# 91 Lord God, you come to us

*Lord God, you come to us:*
*Holy and Trinity;*
*Lord God, you come to us:*
*Creator God.*
*God, Son and Spirit,*
*loves' unique community;*
*Trinity, Unity,*
*Almighty God.*

1. Your act of creation, brought order from chaos,
   you made out of nothing the world that we see
   and, coming in Jesus, in weakness and poverty,
   showed how in splendour love's kingdom would be.
   *Lord God, you come to us:*

2. You poured out your Spirit, creation unfolded,
   you poured out your Spirit, and Jesus was born;
   you poured out your Spirit, a Pentecost dawning,
   poured out your Spirit, the Church came to be.
   *Lord God, you come to us:*

3. One God in three persons, your love in community,
   father and mother of all that exists;
   one God in eternity, God in humanity,
   make and sustain us but dwell in our midst.
   *Lord God, you come to us:*

TUNE: 12.10.12.10.12.11.12.11. Blow the wind southerly
Traditional melody arranged by John Barnard
[Mission Praise Combined 611]

The late Kathleen Ferrier sang this haunting melody in her beautiful contralto
voice and it has been one of my favourite tunes ever since. It is 50 years on 8
October this year (2003) since Kathleen Ferrier died from breast cancer,
robbing the world of her most beautiful voice.

# 92 Mysterious God, your ways unfolded

1. Mysterious God, your ways unfolded,
   Revealed in earthly time and history.
   Men and women you have emboldened
   To speak your truth in life and story.
   *We thank you, Lord, for your revelation;*
   *We thank you, Lord, and praise your Holy Name.*

2. Incarnate Lord, in flesh embodied,
   Enshrined in our humanity you came.
   Human servants called and readied,
   Sent to the world to speak in your Name.
   *We thank you, Lord, for your revelation;*
   *We thank you, Lord, and praise your Holy Name.*

3. Fire of the Spirit, our times are so cold,
   Burst through the gloom in light and love and power.
   Grant to your servants vision to behold
   Your life among us in this present hour.
   *We thank you, Lord, for your revelation;*
   *We thank you, Lord, and praise your Holy Name.*

4. Gracious Father, Son and Holy Spirit,
   We praise and glorify your sacred Name.
   Worship and blessing, praise without limit,
   Past, present, future, always the same.
   *We thank you, Lord, for your revelation;*
   *We thank you, Lord, and praise your Holy Name.*

TUNE: 9.9.10.9. (refrain)　　　　　Genesis
Graham Westcott
[Hymns & Psalms 572(ii)]
[Hymns Old & New Revised 753]

## 93  I live and all the world can see

1.  I live and all the world can see
    just who I am, what I can be;
    So in the universe arrayed
    we see the hand of God displayed.

2.  Sometimes I cause a great surprise –
    an act of love or special praise;
    So in a baby from the womb
    our human nature you assume.

3.  Some acts of service do surprise –
    a different face we recognise;
    In Jesus you surprise us all
    when from a cross we hear your call.

4.  The breath of life is in me too
    to animate the things I do;
    God's Spirit brings both life and love
    as gift and promise, flame and dove.

5.  I try to understand it all
    the self in me beyond recall;
    So can we plumb God's mystery
    with number or with poetry?

6.  So, Lord, I am a unity
    of openness and mystery;
    And how I am helps me to know
    a little of your own credo.

7.  But human nature helps me see –
    that I am one, but somehow three;
    That God, like me, is always One –
    yet always Father, Spirit, Son!

TUNE 88.88. LM                        Herongate
English traditional melody.
Arranged by Ralph Vaughan Williams (1872-1958)
[Hymns & Psalms 224]
[Singing the Faith 415 / 659]
[Hymns Old & New Revised 364]

## 94 Sing a song of joy and gladness

1. Sing a song of joy and gladness,
   to the One who lets things be;
   Mother, Father of creation,
   all that we can know and see.
   *Sing your praises, sing with gladness,*
   *to the Holy One, the Lord;*
   *raise your voices, sing with boldness,*
   *to the first and final Word.*

2. Sing to God who came in Jesus,
   here among us on the earth;
   love alive in words and actions,
   from the cross raised to new birth.
   *Sing your praises, sing with gladness,*
   *to the Holy One, the Lord;*
   *raise your voices, sing with boldness,*
   *to the first and final Word.*

3. Sing to God the Holy Spirit,
   love at work in you and me;
   life and power, joy and freedom,
   setting captive sinners free.
   *Sing your praises, sing with gladness,*
   *to the Holy One, the Lord;*
   *raise your voices, sing with boldness,*
   *to the first and final Word.*

4.     Sing a song of joy and gladness,
to the One in Trinity;
God the Parent, Son and Spirit,
three in one, in unity.
***Sing your praises, sing with gladness,
to the Holy One, the Lord;
raise your voices, sing with boldness,
to the first and final Word.***

**TUNE: 87.87.D**                        **Ode to Joy**
**Ludwig van Beethoven (1770-1837)**
**[Hymns Old & New revised130]**
**[Singing the Faith 8]**
**[Hymns Old & New Revised 183]**
**[Mission Praise Combined 600]**

# 95 In love's unique community

1.  In love's unique community,
    one mind and purpose true;
    source of all life and energy,
    the one who makes things new.
    *We worship you, our love proclaim,*
    *Lord God, we praise your Name.*

2.  The Maker of the universe,
    behind the great Big Bang;
    the mind in which it was conceived,
    the love from which it sprang.
    *We worship you, our love proclaim,*
    *Lord God, we praise your Name.*

3.  The Father who created all
    and Mother who gave birth;
    the Parent of all that exists,
    including planet earth.
    *We worship you, our love proclaim,*
    *Lord God, we praise your Name.*

4.  The love of God came here to dwell,
    incarnate on the earth;
    when in a child at Bethlehem,
    Jesus was born on earth.
    *We worship you, our love proclaim,*
    *Lord God, we praise your Name.*

5.    The Spirit of the Lord at work,
      to make Creation sing;
      the pow'r of love in Jesus Christ,
      the gift of God to bring.
      *We worship you, our love proclaim,*
      *Lord God, we praise your Name.*

6.    So when we sing of Trinity,
      one God our lips proclaim;
      Creator, Parent, Son, Spirit,
      one God our voices name.
      *We worship you, our love proclaim,*
      *Lord God, we praise your Name.*

**TUNE: 8.6.8.6.8.6.**          **Sheltered Dale**
**A German Traditional Melody**
**[Hymns & Psalms 631]**

# Christ the King

# 96 Christ the King of all creation

1. Christ the King of all creation,
   in you heav'n and earth combine;
   God in flesh and blood revealled,
   human and divine assign.
   Born of Mary in a stable,
   crucified upon the tree;
   Christ, the King of all creation,
   comes to set his people free.

2. Christ the King of all our living,
   leads us in loves' chosen way;
   From the cross he speaks forgiveness,
   to the children of the day.
   Crucified, risen, ascended,
   by the Father's side to reign;
   Christ, the King of all our living,
   here we glorify your Name.

3. Christ the King who rules forever,
   him in whom all things cohere;
   Speak the Kingdom Word among us,
   let us now the Gospel hear.
   Take us now with all we offer,
   use us all in Kingdom ways;
   Christ, our King who rules forever,
   may we serve you all our days?

**TUNE: 8.7.8.7.D.**                              **Abbot's Leigh**
Cyril Vincent Taylor (1907-1991)
[Hymns & Psalms P774]
[Singing the Faith 410]
[Hymns Old & New Revised 172, 666]
[Mission Praise Combined 187]

**TUNE: 8.7.8.7.D.**                              **Hyfrydol**
Rowland Huw Pritchard (1811-87)
[Hymns & Psalms 592]
[Singing the Faith 103 / 157 / 568]
[Hymns Old & New Combined 33, 340]
[Mission Praise Combined 226, 315]

# 97 An unknown child in Bethlehem

1. An unknown child in Bethlehem,
   of lowly, gentle Mary born;
   The Saviour of his people comes
   to men and women lost and worn;
   Lord Christ, your Kingdom we acclaim,
   come take, O King, your pow'r and reign.

2. A teacher speaks the words of life,
   to those who feel estranged from God;
   All those far off he gathers near,
   and sinners walk the path he trod;
   Lord Christ, your Kingdom we acclaim,
   come take, O King, your pow'r and reign.

3. When vicious thorns adorned your brow
   and all seemed lost in cruel pain;
   You to the powers of earth submit,
   to their contempt and great disdain;
   Lord Christ, your Kingdom we acclaim,
   come take, O King, your pow'r and reign.

4. The pow'rs of earth had done their worst,
   edged from the earth, nailed to a cross;
   The pow'r of God was still at hand
   to wrest a triumph from such loss;
   Lord Christ, your Kingdom we acclaim,
   come take, O King, your pow'r and reign.

5.   O Christ our King your rule we know
     ascended to the heav'nly heights;
     We come your greatness to proclaim
     your light will banish darkest night;
     Lord Christ, your Kingdom we acclaim,
     come take, O King, your pow'r and reign.

6.   O Christ our King we worship you,
     until your praise fills all the earth;
     Then ev'ry knee to you will bow,
     when high and low proclaim your worth;
     Lord Christ, your Kingdom we acclaim,
     come take, O King, your pow'r and reign.

**TUNE: 88.88.88.**                           **Abingdon**
Eric Routley (1917-82)
Hymns & Psalms 500]
[Singing the Faith 359 / 499]
[Hymns Old 7 New Revised 270]

                                              **Jena (Vulpius)**
Melody by M. Vulpius (c. 1560-1615)
Harmonised by J. S. Bach
[Hymn & Psalms 480]

# 98 Come and sing the praise of Jesus

1.  Come and sing the praise of Jesus
    In a manger born a king.
    Let us follow where he leads us
    Loud and clear his praises sing.
    ***Christ our King your Name we praise***
    ***And with joy our voices raise.***

2.  Jesus worshipped in a stable,
    Lord enthroned upon a Cross;
    Powers of sin and death disable
    Counting all but love as loss.
    ***Christ our King your Name we praise***
    ***And with joy our voices raise.***

3.  Risen Christ, raised up in glory,
    Son of God enthroned on high;
    Let his people tell the story,
    Hear his praises multiply.
    ***Christ our King your Name we praise***
    ***And with joy our voices raise.***

4.  Christ the King of all creation,
    Let all praise and worship be –
    In this hymn of dedication,
    At your Name we bow the knee.
    ***Christ our King your Name we praise***
    ***And with joy our voices raise.***

**TUNE: 8.7.8.7.77.**                    **All Saints**
**Adapted by W. H. Monk (1823-89) from a melody in *Geistreiches Gesangbuch***
**(Darmstadt, 1698)**
**[Hymns & Psalms 60(ii)]**
**[Singing the Faith 725]**
**[Hymns Old & New Revised 828]**

# Remembrance

# 99 Gathered here, Lord, we remember
**Symbol of the poppy**

1.    Gathered here, Lord, we remember
   the great pain and cost of war;
   Still for many to remember
   touches tender nerves still raw;
   Yet the symbol of the poppy
   points to hope most never saw.
   Help us, Lord, as we remember,
   may we strive to end all war?

2.    Gathered here, Lord, we remember
   In thanksgiving what they gave;
   Men and women and the children,
   victims of war, weak and brave;
   Yet the symbol of the poppy
   points to hope beyond the grave.
   Help us, Lord, as we remember,
   may we value all they gave?

3.    Gathered here, Lord, we remember:
   costs in blood and sweat and tears,
   violence, pain and suffering,
   lives were racked with doubts and fears.
   Yet the symbol of the poppy
   points to hope beyond the tears.
   Help us, Lord, as we remember,
   all the cost through passing years.

4.    Gathered here, Lord, we remember
   how the blood of Christ was shed.
   In the very prince of battles
   for the living and the dead.
   So the symbol of the poppy
   points to hope in blood once shed.
   Help us, Lord, as we remember,
   Christ is risen from the dead!

5.    Gathered here, Lord, we remember
      war and suffering increase.
      On the cross Christ fought the battle
      that we all might live in peace.
      So the symbol of the poppy
      points to hope that war will cease.
      Help us, Lord, as we remember,
      let us live in Christ's true peace.


**TUNE: 87.87.D.**                        **Bethany**
**Henry Thomas Smart (1813-79)**
**[Hymns & Psalms 653]**
**[Singing the Faith 25 / 110]**
**[Hymns Old & New Revised  241]**

# 100 We gather in your presence
**A service of memory**

1. We gather in your presence,
   the Lord of all we know;
   the source of earth and heaven,
   our love for you we show.
   You are the same forever,
   time and eternity;
   in past, present and future
   your life and love we see.

2. We gather to remember,
   our loved ones who have died;
   our parents, siblings, children,
   through pain and suff'ring tried.
   To your care we entrust them,
   may love surround them all,
   in joy and great thanksgiving,
   each one we now recall.

3. We gather here to thank you,
   for lives we treasure still;
   thoughts shared and times remembered,
   events and words that thrill.
   We'll not forget this treasure,
   unique and priceless too;
   accept our great thanksgiving
   now offered, Lord, to you.

4.    We gather as your servants,
      met here in sorrow now,
      and in the Name of Jesus,
      before you, Lord, we bow.
      Our loved ones join together,
      upon an unseen shore,
      let praise from earth and heaven,
      sound forth for evermore.

**TUNE: 7.6.7.6.D.**                              **Aurelia**
**Samuel Sebastian Wesley (1810-1876)**
**[Hymns & Psalms 515]**
**[Singing the Faith 690]**
**[Hymns Old & Ne Rvised645, 702]**
**[Mission Praise Combined 126, 640]**

# Harvest and God's Creation

101 Praise the Lord who made the heavens

102 Sing praise to God, who made the stars

103 Our harvest comes round weekly

104 You made the earth, you made the stars

105 Holy God, you made the earth

# 101 Praise the Lord who made the heavens

1. Praise the Lord who made the heavens,
   brought the universe to birth;
   Source of energy and power,
   life and love and faith and worth.
   Praise the Lord of earth and heaven,
   Praise the Lord, who lets things be;
   Praise the Lord, the great Creator,
   Praise the Lord, who sets things free.

2. Praise the Lord, who life unfolded,
   shape and form and beauty flow;
   Stars and planets, living creatures –
   all that through God's love will grow.
   Praise the Lord, who on this planet
   brought all life on earth to be;
   Diverse forms of plant and creature,
   on the land, in sky and sea.

3. Praise the Lord, who in God's likeness
   men and women brought to birth;
   And in Jesus Christ, incarnate,
   lived our life upon the earth.
   Praise the Lord of earth and heaven,
   Praise the Lord, who lets things be;
   Praise the Lord, the great Creator,
   Praise the Lord, who sets things free.

4. Praise the Lord, who calls all people:
   use their gifts, true life release;
   Strive in body, mind and spirit
   to a life of love and peace.
   Praise the Lord, who calls a people
   through the work of Christ on earth;
   Follow him in lives of service
   as God's kingdom comes to birth.

**TUNE: 8.7.8.7.D.**                    **Hyfrydol**
**Rowland Huw Pritchard (1811-87)**
**[Hymns & Psalms 592]**
**[Singing the Faith 103 / 157 / 568]**
**[Hymns Old & New Revised 33, 340]**
**[Mission Praise Combined 236,315]**

# 102 Sing praise to God, who made the stars

1.  Sing praise to God, who made the stars
    And gave the universe its birth;
    The blazing Sun and silver moon,
    The planets and this precious earth.
    All that there is to know and see,
    All things praise God and so do we!

2.  Sing praise to God, who made the earth
    And brought its teeming life to be;
    The plants and birds and insects too,
    And all the creatures in the sea.
    All that there is to know and see,
    All things praise God and so do we!

3.  Sing praise to God, who made 'man' too
    And breathed his life into us all;
    In mind and strength and heart to show
    His image cast in great and small.
    All that there is to know and see,
    All things praise God and so do we!

4.  Sing praise to God, who made us all
    And shared his life with human kind;
    To think and feel, to learn and choose
    To live and love, to make and build.
    All that there is to know and see,
    All things praise God and so do we.

5.  Sing praise to God, who made us all
    And shared our life in Jesus Christ;
    Here in his Name we celebrate
    The wonder of his gifts unpriced.
    All that there is to know and see,
    All things praise God and so do we!

TUNE: 88.88.88.                    **Sussex Carol**
English traditional melody collected and arranged by Ralph Vaughan Williams (1872-1958)
[Hymns & Psalms 364]
[Singing the Faith 148 / 534]
[Hymns Old & New Revised 588]
[Mission Praise Combined 537]

# 103 Our harvest comes round weekly

1. Our harvest comes round weekly
   on supermarket shelves;
   there's mile on mile of good things
   with which to feed ourselves.
   Fruit and veg from all the world
   so we can have our fill,
   and tins, bottles and packets
   all paid for at the till.
   ***These good things around us***
   ***are all signs of God's love.***
   ***Then thank the Lord,***
   ***Yes, thank the Lord,***
   ***for all his love.***

2. O Lord, help us remember,
   in supermarket aisles,
   the goods that are around us
   are more than human sales.
   They are the great provision
   you made for human need;
   for food, for our wellbeing,
   not to sustain our greed.

3. We celebrate the harvest
   that comes in tins and cans.
   We celebrate the goodness
   made real in pots and pans.
   Lord, may we all remember
   your gifts are made to share,
   and not just at our 'Harvest'
   show others how we care.

4.  You show us that our caring
    must have a human face.
    Your love was seen as Jesus
    cared for the human race.
    Help us to show your love now
    to those who are in need.
    That all may know your care, Lord,
    through kindness, not through greed.


**TUNE: 7.6.7.6.D. (Refrain)**          **Wir Pflugen**
**Melody by Johann Abraham Peter Schultz (1747-1800)**
**Arranged by John Bacchus Dykes in Hymns A & M (1866)**
**[Hymns & Psalms 352]**
**[Singing the Faith 130]**
**[Hymns Old & New Revised 801]**
**[Mission Praise Combined 732]**

# 104 You made the earth, you made the stars

1. You made the earth, you made the stars,
   this planet and the universe;
   You made the trees, you made the sky,
   all things that creep or walk or fly;
   ***We praise you for the things you made,***
   ***your greatness all around displayed.***

2. You made the seas and rivers wide,
   the running stream and ocean tide;
   You made the things that dart and swim,
   the fish and all so swift of limb.
   ***We praise you for the things you made,***
   ***your greatness all around displayed.***

3. You made us all, you made each one,
   a process long ago begun;
   You made us male and female too,
   to be creative just like you.
   ***We praise you for the things you made,***
   ***your greatness all around displayed.***

4. You are the One who lets things be,
   the One who set creation free;
   You gave us thought and reason too,
   so we can think and act like you.
   ***We praise you for the things you made,***
   ***your greatness all around displayed.***

5. You are our God, we here proclaim,
   in this our song we bless your Name;
   You are the source of all our praise,
   in worship now our voices raise.
   ***We praise you for the things you made,***
   ***your greatness all around displayed.***

TUNE: 8.8.8.8.8.8.                    Melita
John Bacchus Dykes (1823-76)
[Hymns & Psalms 379]
[Singing the Faith 517]
[Hymns Ol & New Revised 146, 160]
[Mission Praise Combined 122]

# 105 Holy God, you made the earth

1.    Holy God, you made the earth
   You gave the universe its birth.
   Such beauty all around we see
   In plant and animal and tree;
   O Holy God, we sing your praise,
   And joyfully our voices raise.

2.    Creator God, your world around
   Is full of wonder and of sound.
   The mountains large, sands tiny grains,
   The rolling seas, the sweeping plains
   Creator God, we worship bring
   And loud and clear your praises sing.

3.    O Gracious God, we offer thanks
   For all you place in human hands:
   The mind and thought and human powers,
   The precious seconds, minutes, hours.
   O Gracious God, all glory sing
   To you, the Lord of everything.

4.    O Living God, you're still the same,
   In Jesus Christ to earth you came;
   To call your people everywhere,
   To learn to live, your gifts to share.
   O Living God, we're still the same.
   We praise you now, in Jesus' Name.

5.    O God, we come in Jesus' Name,
   In joyful songs to sound your fame.
   We use the talents you have given
   To praise you Lord of earth and heaven;
   For all the wonders of this earth;
   For all that you, O God, gave birth.

TUNE: 88.88.88.         **Abingdon**
Eric Routley (1917-82)
[Hymns & Psalms 500]
[Singing the Faith 359 / 499]
[Hymns Old & New Revised 270]

# A Church Centenary

106   A hundred years of worship

# 106 A hundred years of worship

1.     A hundred years of worship,
    A hundred years of grace;
    A hundred years of blessing
    bound-up in love's embrace.
    We gather here in worship,
    Your Name by all adored.
    We come to sing your praises –
    One Church, one faith, one Lord.

2.     A hundred years of service,
    A hundred years of care;
    A hundred years of living,
    sustained by daily prayer.
    We gather, Lord, to bless you,
    in deeds of love record,
    A people called through Jesus:
    one Church, one faith, one Lord.

3.     A hundred years of preaching,
    A hundred years of time;
    A hundred years of sharing
    your life in bread and wine.
    We learn the ways of Jesus,
    We join in one accord,
    in worship and in mission:
    one Church, one faith, one Lord.

4.     A hundred years of working,
    A hundred years of love;
    A hundred years of seeking
    the ways that God would prove.
    We praise you for the power,
    that takes away discord,
    and binds us in Christ Jesus –
    one Church, one faith, one Lord.

5.   A hundred years of future,
     A hundred years of past;
     A hundred years of living
     in God from first to last.
     We live our lives of witness
     to Christ the living Word,
     and strive each day to serve you:
     one Church, one faith, one Lord.

**TUNE: 7.6.7.6.D.**                    **Thornbury**
**Basil Harwood (1859-1949)**
**[Hymns & Psalms 784]**
**[Singing the Faith 692]**
**[Hymns Old & New Revised 772, 854]**
**[Mission Praise Combined 705]**

# The Opening of a New Church Building

# 107 Lord of ends and new beginnings

1. Lord of ends and new beginnings,
   meet here with us as we pray,
   weave the strands from former churches
   into this new church today.
   Gifts and talents are the treasure,
   that we offer while we sing,
   what is past and all we learned there,
   here in faithful lives we bring.

1. Now we strike out to the future,
   be our guide in days ahead,
   as we make a place of welcome,
   as we gather to be fed.
   As we worship, as we serve you,
   guide us through what Jesus said,
   fill this place with life and power,
   help us his Good News to spread.

2. Gathered here in dedication,
   friends of Jesus Christ the Lord;
   living stones built up together,
   witness to the Living Word.
   Here we offer this new building,
   ev'ry brick and beam and screw;
   bless this Church, our home together,
   bless its life and people too.

3. God, the Father, you have made us,
   Christ, from you all blessings flow,
   Living Spirit, God among us,
   all your fruits on us bestow.
   Blessing to you from all people,
   blessing to the living Son,
   blessing to the Holy Spirit,
   ever three and ever One.

**TUNE: 8.7.8.7.D.**            **Abbot's Leigh**
Cyril Vincent Taylor (1907-1991)
[Hymns & Psalms P774]
[Singing the Faith 410]
[Hymns Old & Ne Revised 172, 666]
[Mission Praise Combined 187]

# Week of Prayer for Christian Unity

**108    Friends of Jesus met together**

# 108 Friends of Jesus met together

1. Friends of Jesus met together,
   one in hope and love we meet;
   seeking the mind of Christ Jesus,
   in his peace each other greet.

2. One in Christ who calls us onward,
   journey with him on his way;
   his the vision of the Kingdom
   that we follow day by day.

3. Friends of Jesus bound together
   seeking for his harmony;
   Christ the one who calls us daily,
   all forgiven, loved and free.

4. One in Christ, the way we travel,
   in his truth and life we grow;
   salt and yeast to all around us,
   as his light in life we show.

5. Friends of Jesus, joined in worship,
   met around the living Word;
   in his Name we raise our voices,
   praise the name of Christ the Lord.

**TUNE: 8.7.8.7.** **Stuttgart**
A melody in C. F. Witt *Harmonia Sacra,* Gotha 1715
Adapted by William Henry Monk (1823-1889)
[Hymns & Psalms 1(i)]
[Singing the Faith 169(i) / 225]
[Hymns Old & New Revised 158]
[Mission Praise Combined 102]

**TUNE: 8.7.8.7.** **Cross of Jesus**
John Stainer (1840-1901)
From *The Crucifixion*, 1887
[Hymns & Psalms 81(ii)]
[Singing the Faith 169(ii)]
[Hymns Old & New Revised 140, 747]
[Mission Praise Combined 607, 683]

# The Baptism of Infants

# 109 Through water and the Spirit

1.  Through water and the Spirit,
    the way of Christ began;
    He came to Jordan river
    to be baptised by John.
    The Holy Spirit's presence
    was in the dove of peace;
    Through water and the Spirit
    began God's masterpiece.

2.  We gather at this font, Lord,
    to share this holy rite;
    Through water and the Spirit
    to share your love and light.
    We come through faith in Jesus,
    baptised so long ago;
    We bring this child so precious,
    [We bring these children precious]
    your truth and love to know.

3.  Baptise her [him][them] with your Spirit,
    this water is the sign;
    Fill her [him][them] with faith and hope, Lord,
    your love with these combine.
    With joy your Church receives her [him]
    your family we are;
    All friends of Christ together,
    drawn here from near and far.

4.     Come, share this time of joy, Lord,
we gather in your Name;
Come, move upon the waters
as we your love proclaim.
Bless child, parents and people,
[Bless children, parents, people]
in all we promise here;
Come fill us with your Spirit,
to know you're always near.

**TUNE: 7.6.7.6.D.**                  **Thornbury**
**Basil Harwood (1859-1949)**
**[Hymns & Psalms 784]**
**[Singing the Faith 692]**
**[Hymns Old & New Revised 772, 854]**
**[Mission Praise Combined 705]**

# 110 Lord, we gather in your presence

1. Lord, we gather in your presence,
   met to praise your holy Name;
   you have brought all things together,
   now we celebrate your fame.

2. Church and parents come together,
   family and friends unite;
   gathered at this place of blessing,
   sharing this baptismal rite.

3. Bless each child we bring here to you,
   each new life brings love and joy;
   when we claim the Spirit's presence,
   may he / she / they all its fruit enjoy.

4. Bless the children here among us,
   nurture them with love and grace;
   help them take the path of Jesus,
   in their lives grant him a place.

5. Bless the parents gathered here, Lord,
   bless each family today,
   as they promise, may they work to
   lead their children in your way.

6. Bless the Church of Christ on earth, Lord,
   arms of love are opened wide;
   joined in worship, love and service,
   may your Spirit be our guide.

**TUNE: 8.7.8.7**
[Hymns & Psalms 251
[Singing the Faith 341 / 382]
[Hymns Old & New Revised 11, 311, 485]

# 111 O Lord, we gather here today

1. O Lord, we gather here today,
   we bring both thanks and praise;
   In love and fellowship we join,
   our hearts and voices raise.

2. We thank you for this precious child,
   so safely brought to birth;
   Lord, you were once a child like this
   and lived upon the earth.

3. We praise you for the love you showed,
   to children, women, men;
   a love you want each one to know,
   right now, as real as then.

4. We bring this infant here today,
   you love him/her as we do;
   Lord, through this rite of baptism,
   we claim that promise true.

5. Then, Lord, we dedicate ourselves,
   to lead him/her in your way;
   To teach him/her the Good News you bring,
   and guide him/her in your way.

6. So may your Spirit bless us, Lord,
   in all we say and do;
   That we may lead him/her as he/she grows,
   to know and follow you.

TUNE: 86.86. C. M.          Gerontius
John Bacchus Dykes (1823-1876)
[Hymns & Psalms 231(i)]
[Singing the Faith 334]
[Hymns Old & New Revised 627]
[Mission Praise Combined 563]

# 112 O Living God we come to you
**Service of Baptism of Infants and Holy Communion**

1.    O living God we come to you
our hearts and voices raise:
With mind and heart and spirit true
we join to sing your praise.
In Jesu's Name we gather here –
the Spirit's power to know –
in words and songs his name revere –
our praises to God show.

2.    Lord Jesus, take the things we say –
in songs and readings too;
Take all the words we speak and pray
that they may honour you.
The praise we offer, Lord receive,
we of your glory sing;
We celebrate what we believe
our praise and worship bring.

3.    Lord God, we gather here today
these children to baptize;
meet with us, living Lord, we pray,
and fill us with your praise.
Come, bless us, Lord, in what we do,
receive these children too;
we dedicate all things to you,
grace all that we will do.

4.    Lord, see your table is prepared –
your own invited guests.
We will receive the broken bread
your presence manifests.
The cup of wine is shared by all,
your cup of blessing know.
As we all share this holy food –
let love within us grow.

5.    O may we walk with you each day –
your presence know and feel?
Lead us, O Lord, along life's way
your pilgrim path reveal.
So, Lord, we give ourselves to you
in worship and in praise;
all that we are we offer you –
your name on high we raise!

**TUNE: DCM.**               **Soll 'S Sein**
**Melody from D. G. Corner [1649]**
**Arranged by John Wilson [1905 – 1922]**
**[Hymns & Psalms 8]**
**[Singing the Faith 53]**
**[Hymns Old & New Revised 320]**

**When Holy Communion is not included in the Service, verse 4 can be omitted.**
**When baptism is not included verse 3 can be omitted**

# Holy Communion and The Eucharist

During 2003, after the Methodist Conference report on Holy Communion was published entitled "His Presence Makes the Feast", I produced a number of hymns to introduce the themes of the report to my congregations at services of Holy Communion. The themes were the nine key themes referred to in the report. These were:

- Thanksgiving — 'he gave thanks'
- Life in unity — 'we are one body in Christ'
- Remembering — 'do this to remember me'
- Sacrifice — 'for you'
- Presence — 'his presence makes the feast'
- The work of the Spirit — 'pour out your Spirit'
- Anticipation — 'the foretaste of the heavenly banquet'
- Mission and justice — 'sent out in his name'
- Personal devotion — 'bread to pilgrims given'.

These hymns are part of the 2003 hymns and the subtitles relate to the above themes.

# 113 We share this meal together

Foretaste

1.  We share this meal together,
    around this table spread;
    For here you bid us welcome,
    to eat your wine and bread.
    *A foretaste of the Kingdom*
    *where each will have a place;*
    *A foretaste of the banquet,*
    *where all will come by grace.*

2.  You have proclaimed the Kingdom,
    the rule of God on earth;
    Where love and truth and justice
    sustain his children's worth.
    *This foretaste of that Kingdom,*
    *this meal of bread and wine;*
    *This foretaste of the banquet,*
    *where all will come and dine.*

3.  We'll follow on your leading
    and walk the Kingdom way;
    And may your Spirit guide us
    in all we do and say.
    *The foretaste of that Kingdom*
    *we celebrate today;*
    *A foretaste of the banquet*
    *that Christ will give one day.*

TUNE: 7.6.7.6.D.                          Wolvercote
W. H. Ferguson (1874-1950)
[Hymns & Psalms 704(i)]
[Singing the Faith 563(i)]
[Hymns Old & New Revised 556, 605]

# 114 Come gather round the table
**All are welcome**

1.  Come gather round the table
    And share this meal prepared;
    Come all of you are able,
    Take Jesus at his word.
    Receive the gift he gives you
    Cloaked in this bread and wine;
    Hear, he is speaking to you –
    He bids you come and dine.

2.  Receive the bread that's broken,
    Christ's sacrifice to share;
    Receive his sacred token –
    Pledge of his love and care.
    Come drink this wine for sharing,
    Christ gives his life for you;
    Come share his cup of blessing,
    The love he offers you.

3.  So gather with his people,
    Responding to his call;
    Know now through word and symbol,
    His love embraces all.
    So met in sweet communion
    With Jesus Christ your Lord,
    You'll know that mystic union
    With Christ the living Word.

**TUNE: 7.6.7.6.D.**                    **Thornbury**
**Basil Harwood (1859-1949)**
**[Hymns & Psalms 784]**
**[Singing the Faith 692]**
**[Hymns Old & New Revised 772, 854]**
**[Mission Praise Combined 705]**

# 115 Take your place, Lord, at our table
**Christ's presence**

1.  Take your place, Lord, at our table,
    guest of honour, priest and king;
    In community we gather,
    here in love and worship sing.

2.  Take the bread we have to offer,
    speak the blessing once again;
    Break the bread as you were broken,
    with your food our lives sustain.

3.  Wine of gladness here we offer,
    bless it as we drink once more;
    As you gave your life up for us,
    through such love our lives restore.

4.  Living Lord, our friend and brother,
    meet with us, our priest and king;
    Here we reach out to receive you,
    faith and hope and love we bring.

5.  As we leave this place of meeting,
    you go with us as we serve;
    Help us, Lord, your way to follow,
    live and love without reserve.

**TUNE: 8.7.8.7.**　　　　　　　　　　**Cross of Jesus**
**John Stainer (1840-1901)**
**From *The Crucifixion*, 1887**
**[Hymns & Psalms 81(ii)]**
**[Singing the Faith 169(ii)]**
**[Hymns Old & New Revised 140, 747]**
**[Mission Praise Combined 607, 683]**

# 116 O Lord, may your blessing rest upon us now
## Leaving blessing

1.  O Lord, may your blessing rest upon us now,
    our time here is finished, it's time to go forth;
    We go in your name, Lord, your Good News to tell,
    you send us to share in your mission on earth.

2.  We thank you for all we've received at your hand,
    your words that inspire us, your loving embrace;
    You called us together, we came from afar,
    we came to your table, we each found a place.

3.  O Lord, by the Spirit you make us all new,
    each fed at your table and transformed by grace;
    We go back to places and people we love,
    yet filled with your vision for all of our race.

4.  So, Lord, we go out in your Name, in your love,
    to serve you in serving, to follow your lead;
    In our daily living, we'll walk in your way,
    and live out our worship in word and in deed.

TUNE: 11.11.11.11.          Normandy
A Basque Carol Melody arranged by Charles Edgar Pettman (1866-1943)
[Hymns & Psalms 45(ii)]
[Singing the Faith 733]

# 117 We rise to leave this holy place
**Sending out**

1.     We rise to leave this holy place,
    fed with the mystic bread and wine;
    Filed with the riches of your grace,
    and clothed in love and power divine.

2.     We held our hands out to receive,
    your broken body in the bread;
    So send us out your cloth to weave,
    that all may know love's finest thread.

3.     The cup of wine put in our hand,
    the cup we share, your love to know;
    We go out now into God's world,
    sent out the Spirit's love to show.

4.     'I will always be there with you' –
    go with us now, your promise true,
    Lead us in ways both old and new,
    let your love shine through all we do.

**TUNE: 88.88. (L.M.)**         **Deep Harmony**
**Handel Parker (1857-1928)**
**[Hymns & Psalms 514(i)]**
**[Singing the Faith 90]**
**[Mission Praise Combined 620]**

# 118 You walked the way of sacrifice

**Christ's sacrifice**

1. You walked the way of sacrifice,
   you lived among us here on earth;
   A humble leader, born to serve,
   to honour God, proclaim his truth.
   And so we praise you, holy Lord,
   our friend and brother, Living Word.

2. You are the one who makes God real,
   to us and those who own your Name;
   You gave yourself upon the cross,
   today as yesterday the same.
   And so we bless you, risen Lord,
   the Easter Christ, God's Living Word.

3. So at the table here we meet,
   the meal that speaks of sacrifice;
   Here in the bread and wine you give,
   we hear again of love's great price.
   And so we thank you, living Lord,
   God is in Christ, the Living Word.

4. From here we go to serve you, Lord,
   to live in love and follow you;
   As we remember all you've done,
   may we live lives that honour you?
   And so we praise you, gracious Lord,
   our friend and brother, the Living Word.

**TUNE: 88.88.88.**                    **Abingdon**
Eric Routley (1917-82)
[Hymns & Psalms 500]
[Singing the Faith 359 / 499]
[Hymns Old 7 New Revised 270]

**TUNE: 88.88.88.**                    **Stella**
Melody from H. F. Hemy's
*Easy Hymn Tunes for Catholic Schools* (1851)
Harmony by Eric Thiman (1900-75)
[Hymns & Psalms 47]

## 119 Your body, Lord, was broken
**One people in Christ**

1.  Your body, Lord, was broken,
    upon the cruel tree;
    This bread is but the token
    of what you did for me.
    We are a living body,
    and live 'in Christ' today;
    One Lord binds us together,
    one life, one truth, one way.

2.  Your life-blood, Lord, was splattered
    upon the tree of death;
    With wine we have remembered
    how life from death sprang forth.
    We are a living body,
    and live 'in Christ' today;
    One Lord binds us together,
    one life, one truth, one way.

3.  You called us, Lord, to meet you,
    to share this bread and wine;
    And here, O Lord, we greet you,
    you meet us as we dine.
    We are a living body,
    and live 'in Christ' today;
    One Lord binds us together,
    one life, one truth, one way.

4.  One people here we gather,
    around your table spread;
    We take the gifts you offer,
    our Lord and living head.
    We are a living body,
    and live 'in Christ' today;
    One Lord binds us together,
    one life, one truth, one way.

**TUNE: 7.6.7.6.D.**                    **Aurelia**
**Samuel Sebastian Wesley (1810-1876)**
**[Hymns & Psalms 515]**
**[Singing the Faith 690]**
**[Hymns Old & New Revised 645, 702]**
**[Mission Praise Combined 126, 640]**

**TUNE: 7.6.7.6.D.**                    **Passion Chorale**
**Melody by H. L. Hassler (1564-1621)**
**as set by J. S. Bach in the *St. Matthew Passion* (1727)**
**[Hymns & Psalms 620]**
**[Singing the Faith 273]**
**[Hymns Old & New Revise 576]**
**[Mission Praise Combined 520, 723]**

# 120 Risen Jesus, fount of grace
**Servants of Christ**

1. Risen Jesus, fount of grace
   here we meet you face to face;
   gathered at your table spread,
   at this meal all will be fed.

2. You have called us to your way,
   "Come and see," we heard you say;
   with the twelve of long ago
   we will follow where you go.

3. Broken body, life-blood shed,
   now you're risen from the dead;
   in this broken bread and wine,
   we receive your life divine.

4. Take us, Lord, your servants now,
   in commitment here we bow;
   walk the streets with us today,
   always with us day by day.

**TUNE: 77.77.**                    **Lauds**
**John Wilson (1905-92)**
**[Hymns & Psalms 326]**
**[Singing the Faith 398]**
**[Hymns Old & New Revised 746]**

# 121 Come and dine, the Lord calls clearly
## Christ's invitation

1. Come and dine, the Lord calls clearly,
   come and share my royal feast;
   all are welcome at my table,
   from the greatest to the least.

2. Bread, here broken to remember
   how I died on Calvary;
   blood-red wine, it is my life-blood,
   shed for all upon the tree.

3. Take the precious gifts I give you,
   here I put them in your hand;
   eat and drink and know my presence,
   here among you all I stand.

4. Saints and sinners find a welcome,
   at this table all are fed;
   food to nurture and sustain you,
   as you follow where you're led.

5. From this table I will lead you,
   into places old and new;
   still my promise to be with you,
   will come true in all you do.

**TUNE: 8.7.8.7.**                    **All For Jesus**
**J. Stainer (1840-1901)**
**[Hymns & Psalms 251**
**[Singing the Faith 341 / 382]**
**[Hymns Old & New Revised 11, 311, 485]**

## 122 Remember the words of the Lord
**Remembering**

1.  Remember the words of the Lord when he said,
    'Meet here at my table, take, bless and break bread.'
    So here, Lord, we gather to meet you once more,
    we each feel your welcome, your table is spread.

1.  Remember how Jesus gave to them the cup,
    'This covenant cup of the kingdom's new wine.'
    So here, Lord, we gather to receive your gifts,
    at your invitation, we come here to dine.

3.  Remember the words of the Lord when he said,
    'I am always with you, I'll always be there.'
    So here, Lord, we gather, your presence is real,
    as we call to mind both your words and your care.

4.  Remember, remember, what Jesus has done –
    his meal at the table, the bread and the wine;
    Remember his promise that he would be here,
    where symbol and presence and love all combine.

**TUNE: 11.11.11.11.**          **Datchet**
George Job Elvey (1816-93)
[Hymns & Psalms 19]
[Singing the Faith 17]

# 123 We bring these gifts of bread and wine
**Offering and receiving**

1.     We bring these gifts of bread and wine,
for you to use, our lives to bless;
You bid us meet, with you to dine,
and in community express –
our life and faith to your design;
Lord, come our lives, our love possess.

2.     We gather round your table, Lord,
as you preside and share this meal;
Come speak afresh your gracious word,
in broken bread your love to seal;
We take the bread you give us, Lord,
through faith and symbol you are real.

3.     We reach our hands out for the cup,
the cup of blessing which you bless;
The cup of sharing lifts us up
and clothes us all in holiness;
We take and drink your loving cup
and feel and know love's warm caress.

4.     So, Lord, we gather at your feast,
that we, with all who love, may share;
We come with all, from great to least,
to taste your gifts and know your care;
Lord, all are welcome at your feast –
a foretaste of your Kingdom's fare.

**TUNE: 88.88.88.**                **Stella**
Melody from H. F. Hemy's
*Easy Hymn Tunes for Catholic Schools* (1851)
Harmony by Eric Thiman (1900-75)
[Hymns & Psalms 47]
[Singing the Faith 516]

## 124 The growing corn stands straight
**Invited guests**

1.  The growing corn stands straight and tall,
    the golden grain is ripening;
    The bursting seeds made into flour,
    from which our gift of bread is made.
    Lord, here is bread for you to use –
    the bread you break for us to share.

2.  The creeping vines grow fast and free,
    with purple fruit are laden now;
    The luscious grapes are picked when ripe
    and made into a rich red wine.
    Lord, here is wine for you to use –
    the cup you give for us to share.

3.  We gather round your table, Lord,
    each won by grace, yet called by name;
    We come, invited as your guests,
    your meal to share, your gifts receive.
    Lord, we are here for you to use –
    the gifts you give for us to share.

**TUNE: 88.88.88.**                **Pater Omnium**
**Henry James Ernest Holmes (1852-1938)**
**[Hymns & Psalms 801]**
**[Singing the Faith 562 / 716]**

**TUNE: 88.88.88.**                **Abingdon**
**Eric Routley (1917-82)**
**[Hymns & Psalms 500]**
**[Singing the Faith 359 / 499]**
**[Hymns Old 7 New Revised 270]**

Walking around the village, indeed travelling to the Gladstone Library at
Hawarden from Manchester, I couldn't help but notice the many fields of
ripening grain. There was the image that became the inspiration behind these
words for use at a Communion Service.

# 125 We hear your invitation
**Christ invites us**

1.  We hear your invitation,
    your call to all is clear:
    'Come gather at my table,
    see you are welcome here.'
    We gather here together,
    we come just are we are,
    Your peace and presence greet us,
    your friends from near and far.

2.  We meet you, Lord, together,
    both young and old draw near;
    This is a time for sharing,
    to hear your message clear.
    We offer love and worship
    and gifts of bread and wine;
    You take and bless and share them,
    give us your life divine.

3.  So gathered at your table,
    we meet with you once more;
    You meet us, feed us, send us,
    to those beyond the door.
    So in your pow'r we'll go, Lord,
    your love will each sustain;
    We'll use the gifts you give us
    as we Good News proclaim.

**TUNE: 7.6.7.6.D.**                    **Thornbury**
**Basil Harwood (1859-1949)**
**[Hymns & Psalms 784]**
**[Singing the Faith 692]**
**[Hymns Old & New Revised 772, 854]**
**[Mission Praise Combined 705]**

# Forster, John Leslie born: 18 July 1944

John Leslie Forster was born in Wakefield, Yorkshire. Following formal education, he trained as an Industrial Chemist with the NCB while studying chemistry on day-release at Leeds College of Technology and Doncaster College of Technology. He obtained an HNC in Chemistry and then studied Advanced Analytical Chemistry. He is a Member of the Royal Society of Chemistry. John was recognised as a Methodist Local Preacher in June 1965. John and Jennifer [nee Sykes] were married in 1968.

In 1971 he was accepted as a candidate for the Methodist Ministry and began training at The Queen's College in Birmingham. During four years at Queen's John became the first Methodist Minister in training to study for an Open University degree. He has been a Methodist Circuit Minister since 1975 serving in the Bilston Circuit where he was also a part-time Industrial Chaplain. Two daughters, Rachel and Sarah, were born while the family lived in the Bilston Circuit. John was received into Full Connexion at the Hull Conference in 1977 and ordained at Chapel Street Methodist Church in Bridlington.

In 1980 the family moved to the Milton Keynes Circuit where John became a half-time Sector Minister [Industry] and minister of Freeman Memorial Methodist Church. During the next six years, John was one of the founder members of CROP [Community Recycling Opportunities Programme] and ran a Community Programme Scheme with the Milton Keynes Christian Foundation. In 1986 John became the Superintendent Minister of the Circuit. He took on significant ecumenical responsibilities with the Milton Keynes Christian Council and was part of the ecumenical team working to building the ecumenical Church of Christ the Cornerstone in Milton Keynes.

The family moved to Middleton in 1991 when John became the Superintendent of the Manchester [North] & Middleton Circuit and part-time Chaplain at North Manchester General Hospital. In the late 1990's the Superintendents and Circuit Stewards of four of the Manchester Circuits met together with the Chair of the District to explore the creation of a Manchester Circuit. This came into being in 2002 with 29 churches. John was one of the two Superintendent Ministers and a founder member of the Superintendency Team. John retired in 2008 after 17 years in north Manchester. He increased his commitment as Chaplain at North Manchester General Hospital to four sessions per week and finally retired in 2012 after 21 years.